Inspirational ideas for pots and plants to transform any garden

THE CONTAINER GARDENER

FRANCES TOPHILL

Photography by Rachel Warne

Kyle Books

To Bilfred and the new little one,
born as I write this

First published in Great Britain
in 2017 by Kyle Books
an imprint of Kyle Cathie Limited
192–198 Vauxhall Bridge Road
London SW1V 1DX
general.enquiries@kylebooks.com
www.kylebooks.co.uk

10 9 8 7 6 5 4 3 2

ISBN: 978 0 85783 380 8

A CIP catalogue record for this title
is available from the British Library

Frances Tophill is hereby identified as
the author of this work in accordance
with Section 77 of the Copyright,
Designs and Patents Act 1988.

Text © Frances Tophill 2017
Photographs © Rachel Warne 2017
Design © Kyle Books 2017

Editor **Vicky Orchard**
Design **Helen Bratby**
Photography **Rachel Warne**
Production **Lisa Pinnell**

Colour reproduction by F1 colour, London
Printed and bound in China
by 1010 International Printing Ltd.

MIX
Paper from
responsible sources
FSC® C016973
FSC
www.fsc.org

WHY SHOULD WE GARDEN WITH CONTAINERS?

I can think of four great reasons:

1. The first is that containers are so convenient. No matter how much, or crucially, how little space you have, containers help us to bring greenery, scents, colours and edibles into our lives.

2. Containers also offer you flexibility in your garden design – you can move pots around or change their contents. This is a great asset; growing conditions that would otherwise be inherently unchanging can be exploited to their full potential. If a plant isn't happy where it is, you can move it – with no disruption! From shade to sunshine or from a windy spot to a sheltered nook. The ability to move a plant is really useful and means you can grow many plants that otherwise might not thrive in your plot.

3. Another obvious benefit is that pots contain the roots of a plant, which is useful for a number of reasons. It might be necessary to prevent a plant from spreading, such as with a bonsai tree or a very vigorous bamboo, or a plant may need a special kind of molly-coddling – such as a very specific soil type that is not present in your garden, extra drainage, or a particularly acid environment (see pages 9 and 136). It also helps to hold roots in a space that is usually inhospitable, giving them the opportunity to feed and hold on against the odds – like on a wall or windowsill.

4. Believe it or not, pots have fantastic design potential. With a host of different shapes, sizes and colours of containers and a whole kingdom of plants to play with, they can add a brilliant and varying aesthetic to your garden. Close your eyes and imagine a pot planted up. I bet I can guess the first thing that popped into your head – the pot was terracotta and had something flowery in it. A *Pelargonium*, let's say. Or maybe it was a hanging basket? Perhaps something with petunias trailing over the sides? The point I am trying to make is that, for some, growing in containers has become something of a clichéd concept. We tend to think of fail-safe, tried-and-tested arrangements. However, there is so much choice and with the further options of upcycling – and even of making your own pots – there really is no excuse for thinking that there's only one way of growing in containers. Think outside the box (or should I say pot?) and try something different.

Plants are good for the soul; they purify the air around us and fill our spaces with pockets of green (one of the most soothing colours), as well as providing havens for wildlife. Plants are also useful – we eat them, we put them in vases, we make dye with them and we use them as the basis for all kinds of medicine. So whatever your space, there really is no excuse for not making a little room for a plant or two. Even just a couple of plants will give you joy and a sense of tranquillity as you nurture them and watch them grow. What better activity is there to do with your children or friends or for a bit of peaceful creative time, than fashioning a container that will be exactly what you want, filled with plants you love?

There is a knack to achieving the perfect container – I've seen some done badly or packed with ill-looking or dull bedding. People tend to revert to the fail-safe option of alternating bulbs in the spring with bedding in the summer, then perhaps some pansies in the winter, if they can be bothered. These sorts of schemes, the types we commonly see planted by councils or in municipal parks, are uninspiring to say the least. But containers need not be synonymous with these kinds of safe and predictable displays. These poor pots, brimming with potential, didn't ask to be filled with the same old species, without colour or form even being a consideration. All that compost, all those nutrients, could have gone to feed and nurture something truly exquisite. There is a whole world of potential to be unlocked from containers that are just sitting in the shed or round the side of the house collecting dust, weeds, moss and possibly spiders and woodlice. I implore you to resurrect, revamp and replant these containers, and this time round, give them a chance to shine. Think of them as the key element of your design, not just a finishing touch or an afterthought. Unleash their true potential.

Fuschia and hardy *Geranium* add flair to a pot display using easily available species.

That's what sets growing in containers apart from all other kinds of horticulture, but there is a whole host of other reasons why you should choose growing in containers over traditional flower beds.

Cost is one; increasingly when we spend money on our gardens, we tend to see gardening as less important and invest in furnishings and hard landscaping rather than plants. Plants can be surprisingly expensive and if they are planted out they generally can't be taken with us when we move – not without some considerable effort and forward-planning, and some may not survive the disruption. Growing your favourite specimens in containers is a cost-effective way of filling your outdoor space while still incorporating some greenery and they can be taken with you when you move. If you have a good-sized space to fill, containers have another clever cost-cutting advantage – because the container adds bulk to the garden, it reduces the need for so many plants to fill the space, and stands in for costly hard landscaping.

Ease is also an important plus for containers. Growing plants in a container is easy – you don't have to do any soil analysis before choosing your plants, you can just choose something you like and stick it into the pot with some multipurpose compost and it will usually grow with relative success. Even trees will be happy in pots for years with some feeding and a bit of water.

Don't confuse ease of planting with being low maintenance. A container plant is reliant on you for survival. In the ground, nature throws all sorts of things at a plant, but if it survives these trials and tribulations, chances are, once it's established, nature will also nurture it. The rain will water it, the leaves falling on the ground will provide it with nutrients and the unconfined earth will give the roots plenty of room to grow. In a container, this is not the case; resources are finite and hard to come by. The designing and the planting process may be easy, but be prepared that maintenance can be considerably more intensive.

By carefully choosing plants that are happy in containers you give yourself less work and less worry. Maintaining plants in pots isn't as onerous as double-digging your vegetable plot or weeding ground elder from your flower beds, they just need a careful eye and an occasional water and feed, and may need potting on into bigger containers when they get too big for their pot (every few years).

You can also grow something in a pot that you might not be able to grow in a flower bed. Some plants need specific soils, light levels or temperatures that your garden cannot provide as when it comes to your garden there is very little you can do to alter the conditions you have. Hence the often repeated phrase: 'right plant, right place'. However, when it comes to containers that rule goes merrily out of the window. You can choose the conditions you want – use an acidic compost for an acid-loving plant, add lime for ones that prefer alkaline conditions, position the pot in a sunny spot if it needs heat. Dig in some gravel to add drainage and compost to help it retain more nutrients, and even move it indoors when it gets too cold. Being able to nurture a plant in a very specific environment is extremely handy, and can be essential to growing that plant well.

I love container growing because of my lack of outdoor space – the good ground I have to grow in is incredibly limited. I am very lucky to have a small balcony when many of us haven't even got that. A patio may be the extent of your 'land', or perhaps just a porch, windowsill, doorstep or even (if you're very lucky) a roof terrace. For the many of us facing this problem, container growing is the ideal solution. Pots fill my windowsills, tables, edges of the bath, desk, doorstep and, quite frankly, anywhere I can shoe-horn

them in. Containers can fit into any space; they can hang from the ceiling, climb the walls, sit on shelves and be incorporated even into the smallest spaces, making them versatile to say the least.

And finally, for those who are lucky enough not to struggle with space, you are in the wonderful position of being able to have some massive containers if you so desire. That doesn't just mean big pots; raised beds are a form of large container, as are walls with growing space at the top, huge urns, installations of every shape or design made of any material you can imagine.

Alpine plants bring greenery with inobtrusive foliage and often delicate and beautiful flowers to almost any area, as long as it gets enough light.

Containers are also invaluable in terms of both plant and garden design. The variety of shapes, sizes, styles and materials combined with the ways in which you can arrange them, where you position them, how you plant around them, how many pots you use, whether you stick to one colour for a sleek, minimalist finish or mix and match them in a shabby-chic, bohemian way, creates almost endless opportunities to create dynamic designs. Add to this the huge choice of plants available and you have a world of options to choose from.

Aeonium of different colours and sizes make a dramatic and architectural centrepiece to an otherwise soft and fairly traditional pot display.

For the more traditional, try terracotta pots filled with bedding plants that are changed in the spring and autumn to give you colour all year round. Or you can use cushion mosses beneath a single coloured plant for impact and an uncomplicated design. Move up the evolutionary timeline towards ferns; try horsetails with striking verticals or the delicate fronds of an asparagus fern for cloud-like texture. You can even do away with the compost altogether and fill containers with water for a hydroponic system or to create an indoor pond. Or if you have walls or stony ground without much soil, you can grow succulents or alpines with shallow root systems to fill every nook and cranny. Or tropical plants in a damp, warm area with rich soil.

There's no end to the combinations you can create with just a little inspiration, but if that seems a little daunting, I'm here to help. In this book I'll show you a wide range of ideas for all tastes to get you growing – but don't forget to do it in your way. Grow the plants you like in your favourite pots so that they give you results that are personal, beautiful, innovative, rewarding and productive in a style that reflects you and your home.

If you've dismissed gardening as something that seems beyond you or your space, it's time to think again. With just a little thought and planning, container gardening can fit into a modern way of life and can be a lot more varied and rewarding than you might expect. So let's get started!

An arid, urban area with poor soil that lends itself to Mediterranean species like olive and thyme is hugely enhanced by some modern herb garden containers for marjoram, hyssop and lavender.

THE POTS

Technically a flower pot is just something that holds the growing medium and the plants. It doesn't have to be a set shape or size or material. It can be something repurposed, something homemade and something you might never even think of as a container. With so much choice, it helps to know your options and which pots best lend themselves to which plants. Armed with all the information, your pot displays can really have the edge.

CHOOSING THE RIGHT SIZE

Generally, containers sit on the ground, or on a hard surface, although don't forget that there is also the option of using a wall-mounted or hanging pot. Wherever you choose to put your containers, when choosing your pot you need to think carefully about what you will use in relation to where it will be situated.

The key to choosing the right container for a specific place is its weight and size. For containers that sit on the ground in a permanent position there are more options, simply because the combined weight of the pot and the compost is not an issue. So on the ground you can create small, dainty arrangements with several little pots gathered together, or use huge raised beds, troughs, urns or any other really large containers.

However, if you wish to put your container on the floor of a balcony or roof terrace, you need to weigh up the options more carefully. A fully finished and watered container is not a lightweight feature – the water alone can weigh a huge amount (1 litre weighs exactly 1 kilogram), but when it is added to a heavy pot filled with compost... you get the picture. The last thing you want to do is over-burden your balcony or roof terrace with weighty items, as this can be very dangerous if the area can't take the load. However, one way of getting around this is by reducing the amount of heavy soil in a container and bulking it up with lightweight polystyrene or something similar. Don't use too much, just enough to make the containers a little less hefty. If you are thinking about a shelf or other wall-mounted system, do bear in mind that you will need even lighter loads and smaller pots.

BIG CONTAINERS

Containers come in all shapes and sizes. I have two large containers in my front garden, in the form of raised beds. This is partly because I cannot grow much in the soil as it is mainly sand and, being near the sea, it has a very high salt content. It also doesn't drain very well (unusual for a sandy soil – lucky me!) so I had no choice but to make two giant containers and fill them with better soil in which I actually have a chance of growing healthy plants.

Many gardeners face the same problems. It could be for all sorts of reasons – whether you have unstable ground, inhospitable ground, trouble bending down to work at a low level, a solid concrete patio that you don't want to break up, a problem with damp soil, or you just like the look of raised beds as opposed to borders dug into the ground. You can get round these issues by building a container to fit your space and serve your needs, and it can be as big as you like or that looks right in your space. It can also have the bonus of doubling up as a seat or storage, with a bit of clever design.

An upcycled metal container makes a bold, modern feature, creating a clever boundary. When softened with a sensitive planting scheme of *Eupatorium* and grasses it looks more rustic.

But for those who do not enjoy building, there are all kinds of large containers available. They can be purpose-built containers, urns being a classic example, or something more contemporary, made of modern materials like concrete or rusted steel. But they can also be something not originally intended to house plants, but cleverly repurposed to do just that. I have even heard of cars being turned into huge containers – plants spilling out of the boot, bonnet and windows. If you have the space, and you love to grow, then a large container does the best job of simulating the ground, as it allows plenty of root space and nutrients. So you can either grow lots more of the plants you love or fewer really mature, large specimens. A big container also makes a bold statement, something that, if you have the courage, can be the making of an outdoor space – even a small one.

Single species make a bold statement. This huge pot is planted with one of the biggest herbaceous perennials – *Gunnera macrophylla*.

A collection of simple,
small pots is a really
effective way of filling
a pint-sized patch and
by using all kinds of
varying textures you
can create something
eclectic, subtle and
undeniably beautiful,
belying your spaces'
diminutive beginnings.

SMALL CONTAINERS

If you only have limited space, don't despair, there is a huge array of containers you can use, as small as you like. There are all sorts of weird and wonderful ideas out there for making containers out of almost any material. The key consideration when using really small containers is the planting, because you need to choose species that can cope with having their roots so restricted. The soil in a small container also tends to dry out and lose its nutrients quicker than that in a large one. So unless you have a lot of time and love to give to your containers, it's worth choosing fairly low-maintenance plants that can cope with dry, nutrient-poor, small spaces, or plants that are extremely slow growing. Plants such as *Pelargoniums*, sedums and other succulents, *Erigeron* and other wild daisies and even many herbs such as lavender, thyme and rosemary can cope with slightly drier, nutrient-poor conditions and, dare I say, neglect from us growers!

As a rule (and a hard and fast one at that), a plant whose roots are restricted will grow slowly. Generally, in containers and in the ground, what's going on above the soil directly correlates with what's going on below. So when the roots are unable to spread and grow, the stems and leaves will be likewise reduced. This is how the Japanese tradition of bonsai works; when the roots of a tree that would ordinarily be tens of metres tall have their growth restricted, the trunk and branches and the leaves are much smaller than they would be in the wild. Be warned that these trees do still need nutrients and a fair amount of water so are pretty high maintenance. However, for those with the time to dedicate to their bonsais (and my dad is someone who puts his all into his collection), a tree can be lovingly nurtured to grow for hundreds of years in one small pot, and never get taller than a few feet (see page 123).

An array of succulent plants in various small containers, proving that there are no limits to the choices you have to make, with clever use of plants. And don't feel limited by these resilient plant species: their shapes and colours can be as varied as the receptacles in which they're planted.

THE POTS

17

CHOOSING THE RIGHT SHAPE

It is an old debate amongst gardeners: a square hole or a round one? I don't think it makes an enormous difference. But in a pot this question has much bigger ramifications in terms of design rather than plant health. And the options are not just round or square but oblong, cylindrical, hexagonal, octagonal, triangular, short and wide, long and thin. The choice is yours but it pays to think about it in advance if you want a cohesive design.

ROUND

Most containers tend to be round – for example, an urn – but even these can be subtly varied in shape, perhaps cylindrical or bowl-shaped. If you want to ring the changes a little, here are a few ideas on how to maximise the impact of round containers.

- Round containers look particularly good when displayed en masse. Round pots are some of the easiest to arrange in large displays and lend themselves to being positioned in corners or indeed in circles.

- Place a large round pot at the centre of a circular piece of paving or deck, or slightly off-centre in a circular feature in your garden.

- Arrange a few pots in a spiral or sprawling cluster; they look particularly good if you use varying sizes of pot, with the largest positioned at the back.

- Generally, circular pots give a slightly rustic look, so they work well in a cottage-garden-style design or something a little more traditional, unless they are cylindrical or columnar, when they can create a striking statement.

It is hard to make square pots look haphazard and they can be untidy-looking unless they are lined up perfectly, either in a diamond formation, as a bigger square or in a straight line. For this reason it can also be hard to combine square and round pots in the same space.

SQUARE

For a more modern-looking design, use square containers. To show them off at their best, try one of these ideas.

- Make them a stand-alone feature in your garden.

- They can be fantastic planted up alongside other square pots, but with a little separation between each container – such as four or five spaced evenly along a wall – or positioned right up against each other to make a continuous line of containers. This can be used to create a boundary or pathway, too.

- Complement their modern look by using architectural plants in a simple planting scheme.

- Use them in a highly formal garden or something with an Italianate twist, or they also look equally good in an incredibly simple design, such as a Scandinavian or minimalist look.

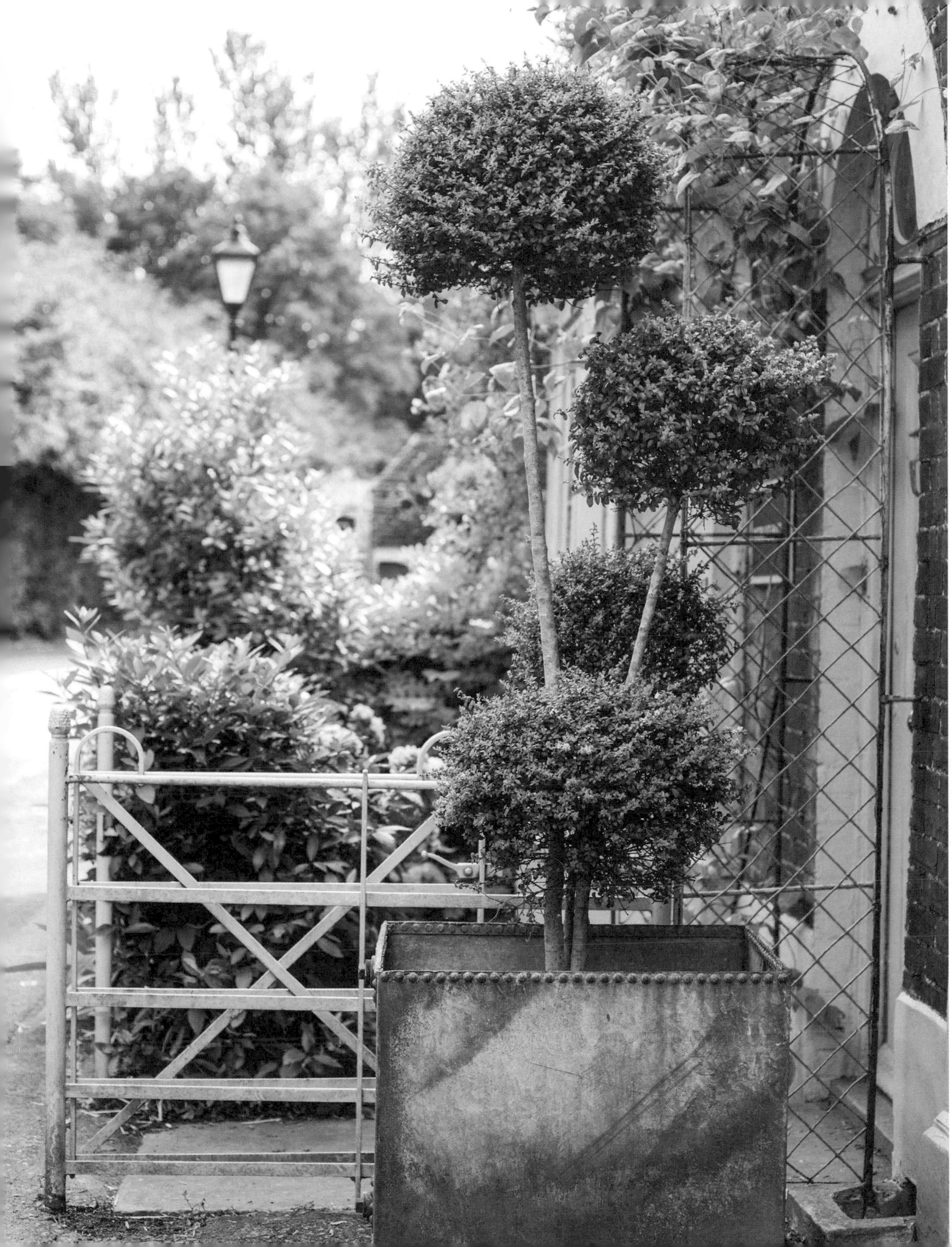

TROUGH

This shape is another common type of floor planter, or as something used on a wall or windowsill. Troughs not only look good but also serve as a sort of raised bed housing lots of plants and maximising productivity. Here are a few ideas to lift the simple to the sensational!

- Troughs make for a great temporary or moveable hedge, either planted up with shrubs or less traditional hedging plants. Try using grasses such as *Miscanthus giganteus* or even sweetcorn as a see-through hedge.

- Troughs are fantastic along a boundary or border to define the edges, or can work as a screen along the edge of a window or balcony, or to hide unsightly parts of the garden such as a compost area or sheds.

- A small, narrow trough is a great option for a windowsill if you have limited space.

- As well as being placed on the ground, troughs can sit on any other hard surface, such as the top of a wall, if properly secured.

- Brighten up the bottom of a boring wall with colourfully planted troughs.

- Use troughs to create pathway edges in the garden, or to separate certain areas of the garden.

- Use them not in a neat line, but staggered for dramatic effect, especially if planted with something tall and architectural.

RAISED BEDS

Raised beds are a step up from the trough and can be made to any height, which can make plant maintenance easier, particularly if you have problems with mobility. These large-scale containers are built up on the ground into any shape from any material you have to hand and can be as complicated or as simple as you like. They are versatile and can fit in with anything from the most rustic designs to the most contemporary statements.

● If you like the rustic look, raised beds can be created by building a dry stone wall, with large stones carefully piled together, and cramming it with cottage-garden flowers tumbling over one another – perhaps even growing through the gaps in the wall, in between the stones. Plants like *Erigeron* lend themselves beautifully to this look. You could give this an even more authentic cottage-garden feel by growing edibles in among the flowers, or perhaps the odd herb. Leave an antique fork sticking out of the soil (for effect, of course – you should never leave your real tools out in all weather!) and you have a stunning traditional cottage-garden bed, all within a beautiful hand-built container.

● The choice of planting is also completely up to you. You can soften the hard edges of the raised bed with tumbling plants, or if you want a minimalist style, then enhance them with single species to create straight lines formed by vertical plants such as reeds or bamboos, or go for something modern and not-in-the-least naturalistic with plants such as mosses, rounded balls of box, tufted grasses or other rounded species such as thrift. The latter in particular go very well with a beach theme.

- A very straight and uniform raised bed gives a completely different look. Made out of wood (see page 84), or concrete or metal, it gives a really modern look.

- If you want a more natural but sleek bed, you could try using railway sleepers. Don't buy reclaimed railway sleepers because of the health risks associated with the creosote they are soaked in, but order new ones that have been pressure treated (also known as tanalised) for an incredibly crisp and fresh look. This kind of timber will turn a pale, washed-out, silver after a few years in situ, but you can also paint it whatever colour you like. Perhaps white-washed for a strong minimalist statement, or try growing something tropical in a deep blue or a vibrant red raised bed?

- Raised beds are also excellent for growing your own and can be filled with herbs and vegetables, or stuffed with flowers for the Romantics, and foliage and greenery for Post-Modernists.

DIGGING DOWN

Digging down into the ground to form a pit-like container enables you to create something different again.

The main thing to remember is that by going deeper into the earth you are more likely to increase the moisture in your container. Water tends to soak downwards in our gardens, and the nearer you get to the water table, the more likely you are to find that your beds are saturated a lot of the time. This can be annoying if you're growing Mediterranean herbs, for example, but you can turn this into an asset, growing plants that are a little specialist and like to get their feet wet. The technical term for something like this is a 'bog garden'. It allows you to grow plants that require permanently damp conditions, such as rushes, sedges, willows, mosses and reeds. There are some plants, such as *Gunnera macrophylla* (which is not allowed to be planted by a real watercourse because it has now been classed as an invasive, and a watercourse allows the seeds to travel downstream and the plant to colonise the natural habitats), that are strikingly architectural but can only survive in the dampest spots. So dig down for a container with a difference.

GOING UP

Wall planters are going up in the world. Many of us suffer from a chronic lack of growing space, so where can we grow? With ever-increasing pressures on housing, the first thing to get squeezed is our gardens. We want to grow plants and reap the associated benefits, and yet we have nowhere to do so.

So what can we do? Well, more and more people are growing upwards. Living or green walls are becoming a lifeline for frustrated would-be gardeners the world over, and mean that you can get growing even if you have only a wall, fence or balcony space. And with the technology in this area getting ever better, there is nothing you can't grow in this way, from delicious produce to colourful foliage and flowers.

The main point to bear in mind if you want to embark on vertical planting is that whatever species you choose must not have a vast spread of roots. You want your plants to grow upwards but not encroach outwards too much; plants have to cram themselves into quite small spaces, meaning they cannot produce too grand a root system.

There are all kind of ways to create a living wall. The simplest is using shelving on which you can arrange pots in any way you like. Put the shelves where you want them, pot up as many containers as you can with your favourite plants and arrange them on the shelves (damp and shade-loving plants for a north-facing wall, and drought/sun lovers for a south-facing one). It might be worth considering securing your shelved pots

in some way to stop them from falling off in high winds. You can tie them onto the shelf, run a wire along the front to hold them in place, or hook them onto the shelf itself. Put screws into the shelves, leaving them protruding by about 2.5cm, then hook the containers on top so that the screw goes into the drainage hole and holds the pot in place.

If you don't fancy shelving and want a living wall where you can't see any of the structure that's holding it in place, there are all kinds of systems you can buy. They do vary in price – some are very expensive while others are relatively modest. It all depends on what you want to spend and how you want it to look.

You can buy professional pocket systems that hang from the wall with pouches ready to be planted. Simply add a little compost, then bed in the desired plants to create an instant green carpet! There are also more inventive, homemade styles that can easily create a beautiful, green backdrop. You can hang pots on strings, create your own pockets using fabric or wood (you can even fashion your own green wall out of wooden pallets (see page 78), or exploit existing cracks in brickwork by using them as planting holes. If you use one of these

methods, be sure to choose plants that can cope with very dry conditions because you don't want to damage your brickwork by adding too much water to it! If you have a strong, solid wall or fence you could screw pots to it and plant them up.

For the more adventurous there are countless ways to create a living wall if you are prepared to make something yourself. Hanging pots, making living frames and putting them up, screwing pots to walls are just a few options, and I will go into more detail about these methods in the projects chapter, but suffice to say there are lots of methods for making your planting go upwards and encouraging greenery in places you might not think possible

HANGING BASKETS

When we think of containers, we often think of hanging baskets. These are wonderful when seen in their full glory and are a firm favourite among gardeners keen to maximise their planting spaces. The key consideration with a hanging basket is the plants. Get the wrong plants and the whole effect will be ruined.

A basket like this is stunning. It takes over 30 plants to create and regular feeding but the results are well worth the effort.

This is not the case for most containers, but the reason why you need the right plants for hanging baskets is because usually they have to hide the often not-aesthetically pleasing container, so you want plants that hang down to cover the sides and so that they can be seen from below. This is why you often find plants like petunias or fuschias in hanging baskets, as they effectively perform both of these tasks, as well as producing a pleasing scent, all in one growing season. They are also fairly cheap. But you can be much more adventurous than sticking to petunias, as there are other plants, both ornamental and cropping, that will also perform very well in a hanging basket (see page 82).

But don't just focus on the plants if you choose a hanging basket; think about the container, too. You are spoilt for choice,

both in terms of containers designed for hanging and also rethinking or upcycling an existing item. Bird cages are a classic example of an item that can be repurposed into a hanging basket. Any object that can be hung can make an effective feature when enhanced with plants. And there is not even always a need for soil; for the more adventurous gardeners there are water plants and air plants (see page 106) that get all the nutrients they need from gas exchange or having their roots in water. Orchids are a prime example; many of these plants naturally grow in trees and get their nutrients from the air around them. Using these types of plants can make a really interesting hanging basket, and excluding soil can be ideal where weight is an issue. If you choose to grow orchids like this, chopped cork makes an excellent growing medium.

WINDOW BOXES

Like hanging baskets, window boxes can have a questionable reputation. Sadly, we have been all too frequently exposed to plastic window boxes – cheap plastic at that, possibly in green or imitation terracotta, or white. However, there is no reason why this should be the case. If a traditional plastic window box is all you have and your budget won't stretch to a terracotta or metal trough-type one, you can easily give it a makeover using paint, découpage, or by gluing on textured surfaces (see pages 146-151).

Plant it up with whatever takes your fancy – large or small, permanent or seasonal. Whatever it contains, whether bulbs such as daffodils or tulips, or herbs such as thyme, basil and parsley, or even a wildflower annual mix that brings the bees buzzing to your window, a container like this will bring beauty and joy every time you look out of the window.

MATERIALS

If you grow in containers in a considered way, then the choice of pot should be likewise deliberated. It is far too easy to go to a garden centre and pick something based on ease, price and convenience, but I urge you to plan and think about which material best lends itself to the kind of feel you want to create in your outdoor space. And don't forget colour. White can be modern or traditional, dark colours create a definite look and bright colours can be exotic or can verge into the childish if not used carefully.

There are ways of changing the look of something, or playing with its inherent qualities, either modern or otherwise, by offsetting them with something contrasting (a flowing cottage-garden scheme in a steel container for example), but to guarantee a cohesive look, it is safest to choose a theme and stick to it. This includes the materials of your containers.

PLASTIC

We all know about this material. No matter what it is used for, it cannot really be called beautiful. Plastic pots have never been the height of horticultural fashion, but nowadays there is a much wider range to choose from, which makes plastic pots more desirable. There are also many ways that you can make them more aesthetically pleasing with just a little wherewithal and imagination, including decorating them with découpage, sand, paint, rope, shells, transfers or mosaic (see pages 146-151 for ideas).

But rather than thinking of plastic containers as a fashion faux pas, remember the benefits of this material – there is more to say in favour of the plastic pot than it may at first appear.

- The first advantage of the classic plastic pot is that it is cheap. You really can't go wrong with one for basic growing, if aesthetics aren't your main objective. You can pick them up almost anywhere for next to nothing, and for the thrifty, those in the know and those who are into free-cycling or recycling, they can often be obtained second-hand or for free. There's a lot to be said for that in a world where everything always costs more than you might think – especially an all-singing, all-dancing container.

- The second big pro for plastic containers is that they come in a vast range of shapes, sizes and colours – with drip trays to match. You can also get seed trays, 7cm pots, 9cm pots, cells (which are also for growing seeds but in their own separate compartment, usually for larger seeds) and plugs. For mass growing and for easy growing, plastic really is the best option.

- For the plant-lovers out there, a big plus for plastic is that the pots are designed to be really effective at growing plants. That might sound silly, but having worked in nurseries that tried to use alternative materials, we found that there really is no more reliable receptacle for getting plants going. The drainage holes are the right size for holding on to the optimum amount of water while also allowing the pots to release enough liquid to prevent plants becoming waterlogged. The shiny surface of plastic also means that it doesn't crack in cold weather, the pots can be stacked easily and can be stored en masse without too much hassle, and they are light, making them easy to transport – even with a plant growing in them.

As an idealist, if someone were to present me with a pot that was as cheap and effective at producing healthy plants as a plastic one, and that was not detrimental to the environment, I would bite their hand off. But gardeners are also pragmatists; we like to grow plants that will survive and will go on producing for us, without being hampered by bad material. So when needs must, we use products that may not be as carbon neutral and ethically sound as they could be. I personally do not advocate this and so I do try to minimise my use of plastic pots (as well as avoiding spraying chemicals wherever possible and using peat-free compost). For those, like me, who think about these issues, there are now well-supported schemes set up to recycle and reuse plastic pots. I urge you to look these up and to use them wherever possible. That way, the more we grow, the more we reduce our carbon footprint.

The nice thing about wood is that it gives you versatility in terms of design. You can go for a very rustic and earthy look by using materials like driftwood (collected with permission from your local authority and environmental groups) or reclaimed materials such as scaffold boards or similar.

WOOD

When it comes to wood, there is plenty of scope for creating your own, bespoke containers, and there are also many lovely existing designs.

● The humble wooden container also complements more formal garden designs. Traditionally this style is known as 'Italianate', meaning that they are designed 'in the Italian (Renaissance) style', although actually they are now more typified by British and French gardens. So much so that one of the leading lights in traditional wooden containers has been named the 'Versailles planter' – which is a square vessel, often decorated with little balls at the top of each corner post. These smart planters give a grand feel, but they are also practical, as the traditional designs can slide apart to make repotting, feeding and renewing compost, as well as tasks like dividing plants, a little easier rather than having to dig or tip out the contents of the container.

● There is also a big 'but' with wood, and that is that it rots. You can buy wood that has been pressure treated, which will have a considerably longer life expectancy than untreated, but generally this does not make the most attractive timber. So the compromise is that you will have to periodically treat your exterior timber with preservative or, occasionally replace all your exterior timber once it begins to age. However, this deterioration can take a good number of years so don't write off wood as too high maintenance, it is a wonderful, versatile and – if ethically sourced – environmentally sound material.

Alternatively, you can choose a finish that is more refined and genteel. Planed and smoothed hardwoods (any deciduous species like oak or chestnut) make the perfect surface for your plants to dangle against in raised beds. You can also buy a pre-fabricated container in this wood, or for a really sleek finish, you could build the planters into the rest of your hard landscaping, incorporating them into raised decking, for example, or to act as dividing walls.

33

There is a vast range of choice when it comes to clay. The colours can vary, the shape, the size, the style and, unlike most other kinds of pots, there are actually some more functional options available. Tragically for those of us who try to be a little thrifty, clay pots have become artisan items and often come with a high price tag. However, there are still bargains out there. I recently picked up a load of clay containers from a friend who'd closed her nursery business. She had hundreds of small terracotta pots that she wanted to get rid of, so I have given them a happy home.

STONEWARE + EARTHENWARE

Clay containers are an extremely popular choice. The word 'pot' itself, which is so frequently used to describe containers, comes from the word 'pottery', and there are many good reasons for this material being an old favourite.

- The first is that it is so hardwearing; it can cope with heat, cold, wet, dry, wind, rain and basically any condition you choose to throw at it. There are some clays that might crack in very cold and wet weather, because water that has soaked into the pores expands as it freezes, but generally a clay pot will be able to withstand most, if not all, weather conditions.

- A great way to get inspiration is to look at your neighbours' houses and gardens to see what they have, and then ask them where they got their pots. It's also a nice way to get to know your neighbours – though don't blame me if you regret this later!

- You may remember the blue pots that dominated TV screens and garden centres for many years, and I still have a soft spot for them. I love the rich colour of lapis lazuli, but glazes come in such a variety of shades that there is plenty of choice. Have a look in your local garden centre – their range will be just the tip of the iceberg. There are now shops that specialise in pots of all kinds and there are also some small independent potteries that produce containers, sometimes to order, and often for surprisingly little money. So shop around in your local area and see what you can find.

Even just a small selection of the clay pots available shows the variety of choice for all colours, shapes, sizes and positions in the garden.

I would not normally recommend a plantless container but will happily make an exception for fire! If a fire pit is something you want in your garden, and after all this is essentially a container for fire, then stone is the ideal material for this. Metal is really the only other option.

STONE

Unlike terracotta, stone pots tend to put greater weight on aesthetics rather than practicality – in other words, don't look for little versions to grow your seedlings in. But stone pots are usually very beautiful.

- They come in both rustic and extremely modern forms, and there is currently a movement towards the marble-like but matte-finished carved pots – the likes of which would have graced the Parthenon – but without the fussy decoration. Stone containers tend to be on the large side, too, and this craftsmanship and scale often come with a hefty price tag.

- However, there is no denying that the beauty of a carved piece of stone is captivating and gives importance and weight to a garden design. Because of its potential size and grandeur, a stone container can feel like part of the furniture, part of the very make-up of the space and can help to bring together a design – for example, to blend in with or complement hard landscaping such as a patio or walls, so the containers feel like part of the design rather than an afterthought.

- There is no need to stick rigidly to this way of using stone. The rustic look never goes out of fashion if it looks intentionally rustic, and there is always a huge range of such containers to choose from. These are often smaller than their elegant, smooth equivalents, which makes them an ideal choice for a more modest-sized garden.

- If the price of real stone makes this option unfeasible, there are lots of more modestly priced, concrete alternatives. Many of these are made from direct casts of their stone counterparts, so to all intents and purposes they look just the same.

If you want to really integrate stone containers into your garden, why not build them yourself? You can make containers in walls by leaving a gap for planting on the top surface. If you are building the walls yourself, or having them built by a builder or landscaper, you can design them however you like – in any colour, texture, shape, width or height. You could make them smooth and modern, or rustic, or even use a dry stone wall both to contain your plants and use the little crevices between the stones to grow other small plants.

However you plant them up, containers made from bricks or stone provide a fantastic opportunity to seamlessly incorporate plants into the design, and also to use them for what designers and gardeners have been using them for for centuries – to soften the hard lines of landscaping materials.

METAL

Metal is an increasingly popular choice for containers. It can come in a range of shapes, sizes and colours and gives an industrial feel and a modernist look. But metal can also be a beautiful and unpredictable material as it ages, reacting with the elements to form bubbles, imperfections and bold colours.

If you buy a metal container because of the way it looks at that time and want it to stay that way, there are many metals that will remain crisp and fresh in appearance. And (let's get down to the really dull stuff) they are really easy to clean. So if that's more appealing to you, ask for galvanised steel which will not weather at all. There are some really cheap bucket-style containers and other pots made of metal that are quite utilitarian, and a good alternative to plastic, without being overpriced. They also give an upcycled look without you actually having to do any work at all.

The brilliant thing about many metals is that they age so attractively; as the seasons pass and the weather has its effects, they change colour and patina, and unlike many other materials, often improve with age. The obvious example is iron, which turns a vivid burnt orange, but think too of copper steeples on old churches and their gorgeous, aged-green colour, or the russet hues of oxidised brass.

If you are a fan of the aged metal look without necessarily liking its capricious nature, you could look into containers made from corten steel, which has a uniform rusting effect that looks both modern and aged. It's becoming increasingly popular and is well worth investigating.

Another advantage of metal is its magnetic quality, and you can buy magnetic pots. They aren't cheap, but they are pretty amazing. This material is great used as mini herb-growing containers that can be stuck onto the fridge or to metal walls or other surfaces in the garden (see page 96). This allows you to make a really simple living wall without having to drill in brackets and frames, so the pots can be easily replaced or revitalised throughout the year, when they grow too leggy, or just when you feel like a change. It also gives your living wall the flexibility for pots to be moved according to how well the plants are doing; if one plant is being hammered by the wind, you can move it to a lower position. Or if a plant is being affected by the shade, you can move it up so it gets more sun.

If you're using a metal container that will age, always remember to treat the inside so that rust does not turn the soil too acidic. And drill some holes in the bottom!

GLASS

You might not immediately think about putting glass containers in your garden (we naturally think of glass as being delicate and brittle), but its merits are becoming increasingly appreciated and, when you think about it, that makes perfect sense. We have used glass in the garden for centuries – as cloches, greenhouses, cold frames and many more features.

- These practical uses have become quite outmoded, but I believe that we should use glass as a staple material for outdoor growing. Glass is strong, and with reinforced or toughened glass, it is becoming even more versatile. If you have small children, though, think carefully about covering your garden with glass containers – particularly if they are not made from toughened, shatterproof glass – but otherwise there should be nothing stopping you from using it.

- Glass is not as strong as stone, or as flexible as metal, but it is not much different to clay in its make-up and has one very interesting quality that clay does not – it is clear. This opens new doors for growers in terms of the species they can grow and the look they can achieve.

- We tend to use containers in a fairly single-minded way: we fill them with compost and grow plants at the surface. This is because if we put the plants too deep in the pot they miss out on a key requirement – light. So materials like clay limit your growing capabilities, unless you're using it for a very specific purpose, such as excluding light to force rhubarb in the spring. With glass containers this problem is eliminated; your containers can become miniature glasshouses. This creates a mini microclimate; the light lets in heat in the form of reacting photons (particles of light), which increases humidity and allows you to grow plants outside that you could never have grown before, including tropical and subtropical species.

- With modern-day sustainability in mind, this leads us onto another reason for using glass containers – and that is as a means of recycling. We get through so much glass in our homes: as bottles and jars for beer, wine, jam, honey, water and other drinks, or for spices and herbs. You can recycle these items in specialised centres or in the correct recycling bin, but you could also reuse them in a slightly more creative way by upcycling them. Used in this way, old glass can make beautiful and very simple containers, either traditionally as pots, or as terrariums, and make great gifts.

- If the clarity of the material is a good reason for using glass, then I'd like to advocate clarity of the substrate, too – the compost substitute. Many plants grow simply in water, from which they can get

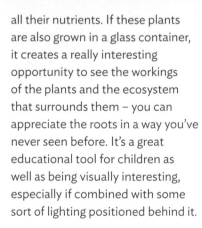

all their nutrients. If these plants are also grown in a glass container, it creates a really interesting opportunity to see the workings of the plants and the ecosystem that surrounds them – you can appreciate the roots in a way you've never seen before. It's a great educational tool for children as well as being visually interesting, especially if combined with some sort of lighting positioned behind it.

- And for those practical growers out there, don't think that growing in water and glass is reserved for weird and wonderful water-loving species – many edible crops like lettuce, leeks and onions can be grown in just water. Simply leave the roots intact, or the base of the plant if there are no roots left, and stick them in an old jam jar on the windowsill.

POND POTS

Container ponds can be any shape, size or style that you want them to be. They can be made from pots or tanks, made of plastic, glass, metal, brick or stone and be square, round, hexagonal, sunken, raised. They can be all these things and still be great for wildlife, if you want an informal theme, or as more modern-looking features. Having a pond pot also provides the opportunity to grow a whole range of water-loving plants that you couldn't ordinarily grow in a run-of-the-mill container.

GROUPS OF POTS

Using lots of containers together is a very traditional yet incredibly effective way of displaying plants. This type of container gardening has had somewhat of a renaissance in recent times, but with a slightly different spin. And the group does not have to be two-dimensional; using containers of differing sizes and shapes, and platforms to elevate the ones at the back, you can add height and even multi-layers to your display, which is a great design tool, especially in a small space.

- One simple way to create temporary impact in a garden that can be repeated in your next garden, if you move, is to group together a tasteful display of three or maybe five pots (always work in groups of odd numbers). The pots could be the same colour (or shades of the same colour – see left) or a variety, depending on the look you want to create, and usually look best in a variety of sizes.

- Plant them with minimal, usually monochromatic (green and one other colour) planting for a tasteful display. Red and green create a bold statement, whereas green and pastels like pale blues, pinks, lilacs, soft yellows or white, create something more subtle. You could even choose green and a paler green for something ultra modern, or green and black (or as near black as can be in the plant world – usually a profoundly dark purple) for a striking look. Herbs such as thyme and rosemary look particularly lovely, as well as being tasty and evergreen to boot!

Here retro '90's blue glazed pots en masse have been given a new lease of life with some bold, bright flowers.

For more confident and adventurous plants, move away from monochrome and into multicolour. Here, a tropical feel is created with *Canna*, *Dahlias*, *Cercidiphyllum*, *Fuchsia*, *Salvia* and *Hosta*, using complementary foliage and flower colour.

With patience, a truly
breathtaking collection of
pots can be created using
a huge range of species.
Great for plant collectors.
And when a plant goes over,
simply replace it!

HOW TO...

Get the groundwork right, and growing in a container is easy. Mostly planting in a pot is common sense, but there are a few tricks of the trade that will make your plants infinitely happier in their little homes and this, in turn, will make looking after them much easier.

In this chapter I will take you through the different stages of creating your containers, and the different options you might choose at each stage to make your pots both serviceable and stunning.

FIRST THINGS FIRST: THE POT ITSELF

Think of a container as its own little ecosystem. You have the ground (that's the compost), the animals (the microbes, worms and bugs that live in the compost) and the plant life (whatever you choose to grow in your pot). In a normal ecosystem these components are infinitely complex, ever-changing and bigger than you will find in your mini, container-sized ecosystem. In a garden you get an idea of what it is to create a real habitat with complex, numerous layers of organisms acting with and upon each other, creating a fluctuating world that more or less takes care of itself. This is not so in a container, and that is the main thing you need to understand if you want to be a successful container gardener – particularly when it comes to nurturing your plants.

The basic principle of container gardening is that you are taking a small part of an ecosystem and isolating it. You might have patches in your garden that are shady, sunny, dry, damp, windy, sheltered, frosty in winter, protected in winter and every variation in between – all in the one space. In a container this is not the case; you have little to no diversity. If you have a container that suits a drought-tolerant plant, then every plant in that pot must be drought tolerant. In this sense, particularly for beginners or those who like to keep things simple, this makes your job easy. On the other hand, the lack of natural fluctuation removes a certain degree of the force of nature. In a monoculture or overtly simplified mini ecosystem you lack the natural build-up of nutrients you would find in a wild ecosystem. Similarly, there will not be as many worms and microbes to enrich the soil. Remember reason number two in chapter 1: You can always move a container if it's not doing well!

The big positive is that in a container you have ultimate control over what you grow and where. However, you also have a big responsibility because the survival of that plant in that pot depends almost solely on you. So how do you get this unique relationship between pot, plant and person to thrive? Well, there isn't one easy formula, essentially it is up to you to provide the optimal conditions.

There are five key things that every plant needs to survive:

- Water (in varying amounts).
- Air (both above and below the ground).
- Nutrients – different requirements for different plants, but essentially the same 12 nutrients in different measures (see page 56).
- Temperature (different temperatures for different species).
- Light (again in varying amounts).

The first thing to consider when choosing or making a pot is its size. This is key for whatever plant you want to grow. Certain plants like *Agapanthus* and strawberries need very little root space and can cope well with their roots being restricted, while others like figs and hops will accept being in a pot but would really do better in the ground. In such cases, the bigger the container the better. But remember, the pot must also fit in the space you have.

Once you have thought about these things you should have a rough idea of the size of pot you need. If you have the container already and have assessed its size, you need to decide what kinds of plants you can put in it. For instance, if you have just discovered a tea tin for less than the price of a cup of tea in a charity shop, you're not going to try to wedge an apple tree into it – that's just common sense. You might be thinking about going smaller, more compact, perhaps along the lines of some pea shoots, watercress, herbs or a strawberry plant. If you're more into flowers, an alpine like a saxifrage or *Raoulia* would do very nicely.

If you do have a huge urn or a trough, you can use it for a much larger plant – perhaps even a tree. A Japanese maple makes a nice feature for a container, or try growing a cherry, plum or pear if you're keen to grow your own fruit. Or – and this is where there is almost endless opportunity for flair and creativity – you could fill the pot with a whole host of different species to make a beautiful display. Flowers of complementary colours and similar predilections live in harmony in one container, or if you're partial to a more restrained palette, you could have differing species in just a single colour. Or even (for the minimalists) you could fill a large container with one species for an unfussy, clean, muted look.

MATERIAL

The second consideration is the material that your container is made from. There is a slight difference in which plants suit which materials.

PLASTIC with its shiny surface, this is really good for plants that like high levels of moisture, because it holds in water, not allowing it to seep through the sides.

TERRACOTTA (unglazed) works well with species that like free-draining soil and cope well with hot roots, as the pores in the material allow water to be released and keep the soil cooler. If the terracotta is **glazed** – especially if it's glazed on the inside – it doesn't allow for seepage and so will be much better for water lovers.

METAL is a tricky material for a container, even though it may look great, because of its tendency to get extremely hot in the sun. There are few, if any, plants that really enjoy having their roots get this hot. For example, a clematis will simply turn up its toes and refuse to flower if the roots begin to bake. However, there are some plants, often corms (specialised storage roots a little like bulbs), that 'need baking' in order to flower, and these are usually planted with their roots exposed to the sunlight. Flag irises are a classic example of this. These sorts of flowers cope in a metal container as long as there is enough soil between the metal edge and the roots themselves. But, generally, if you really want to use metal containers, it is wisest to put another (preferably plastic) container inside the metal one to reduce the amount of heat conducted through the soil, thus protecting the plant inside.

WOODEN containers are fairly versatile, but as they are usually lined with a plastic or butyl liner to prevent the wood rotting, they do lend themselves to plants that like to get their feet wet. However, armed with a drill, you can pierce several drainage holes into the base of the liner to make them good receptacles for plants that prefer drier conditions.

There are, of course, containers available that are made from many other materials that are too numerous to list here, but I've tried to cover the most common types. Whichever material you use, be are aware of one key requirement: drainage holes.

DRAINAGE

Drainage is a very important part of container gardening. More plants are killed through over-watering than under-watering, especially in today's unpredictable climate. So it is crucial that your containers get the right amount of water.

Generally, with most plants, you need to include at least one large, or several small, drainage holes in the base of your container. Think of the standard black plastic pot that your plants come in from the garden centre, which have several holes in the bottom – that gives you an indication of how well drained most plants need to be. And ugly and environmentally unfriendly as those pots may be, they are arguably the most effective receptacles for growing plants.

It is important to get the right amount of drainage for specific plants, so be aware of the needs of the plants you are using. There are many plant species that need a lot of water; for example, bog gardens have become increasingly popular in recent years, encouraging people to grow plants that thrive in a waterlogged or permanently moist environment. If you decide to make a bog-garden container, put one small drainage hole in the bottom, just to make sure the soil doesn't get completely waterlogged and toxic. But make no more than one, otherwise the drainage will be too effective and therefore unsuitable for the species you want to grow. If you are making a pond in a pot, there is no need for any drainage holes at all. In fact, if you do put them in, rather than a glorious haven for aquatic plants, you are more likely to get a claim on your house insurance, or the downstairs neighbour's, when the contents flood out!

CROCKS

Another good way to improve drainage is by using crocks, or crockery. This is the stone, polystyrene or, more commonly, broken-up bits of pottery that go in the bottom of your container before you add the growing medium.

How many bits of crocks you need depends on the conditions that your plant prefers. Obviously the more drought tolerant your plant is, the more crockery it will need in the container, but even moisture-loving plants should have a few bits in the base of the pot, as it serves to stop the build-up of wet, sloppy soil, full of pathogens and toxicity due to waterlogging. No plant likes that kind of moisture; even in a pond you will need to include oxygenating plants to get air to the roots of the aquatic plants. A sloppy base of soil will do nothing but harm. So sticking a few stones or a bit of broken pottery in the base gets the water moving through the soil quickly once it gets down to a deeper level in the container. It can also cover the holes in the pot to make the soil inside less likely to fall through the drainage holes when you water. So it's win-win.

COMPOST

The next consideration (and now we are really into the nitty-gritty) is the compost that you use. This is where things start to get a little more complex. Unlike all the other steps, it is not just a case of choosing your soil and letting the plants get on with it. Whatever growing medium you choose will need to be replenished on an annual or biennial basis to keep plants thriving (see page 152).

In technical circles we use the term 'growing medium' or 'substrate', rather than soil or compost, simply because a lot of plants don't necessarily like a soil-based medium. The pond in a trough (page 106), for example, uses water as its substrate, whereas something like an orchid grows best in chopped up cork. Get the substrate right and you are more than halfway to success. If in doubt, consider it a general rule that most plants like a neutral to slightly acidic compost.

COMPOST TYPES SIMPLIFIED

Acid-lovers	Ericaceous compost
Edibles (fruit and veg)	Nutrient-rich compost (with manure)
Edibles (herbs)	Free-draining compost with sand or gravel added
Seeds and cuttings	Low-nutrient compost
Conifers	Slightly acidic compost
Water-lovers	Humus-rich compost
Aquatics	Water
Orchids	Cork or bark
Cacti, succulents and drought-lovers	Free-draining compost with lots of sand or gravel

Compost mixes can create something of a row. For many generations we have used peat as our principal growing medium, for a number of reasons. First, it is really good at retaining moisture without getting waterlogged. Second, it is low in nutrients, which means that you can add whichever nutrients the particular plants you are growing will need, tailoring it to their exact requirements. There are, however, some rather dramatic drawbacks to some compost blends. Peat is an endangered and ever-decreasing material; peat bogs take thousands of years to form and are unique environments, and despite much research, scientists are finding it impossible to recreate the conditions in which peat develops. The bottom line is that we are eating into a finite resource when we add peat to compost, so it is worth being aware of the peat-free alternatives that are available. I always try to use these wherever possible.

However, there are also objections to some of the alternatives. Coir, for example, is a really good, peat-free growing medium that is a waste product from the coconut industry, but it is often associated with less-than-fairtrade working conditions and, of course, high air miles.

Another, fairly obvious, alternative to peat is a soil-based compost. This is a great option as you can produce it yourself by mixing your own garden soil or bought topsoil with compost and leafmould (composted leaves), which makes it a cheap option. The only drawback is that its drainage levels vary, depending on what type of soil you have or the kind of soil-based compost you buy. You may have to improve the drainage by adding something from the 'soil additives' section (see page 54).

Something that I use a lot, and find really good as a basic container growing medium, is a compost made from bulrush. It's light and free draining and it grows healthy specimens. It is a really good alternative to peat as it is a completely renewable resource.

So there you have the minefield that is choosing your growing medium. Now what do you do with it?

ADDITIVES

There are many substances you can add to the compost at this stage of planting up your container that will make your plants healthier and, crucially, make your life easier in the long term. So what are these additives and what do they do?

GRAVEL OR SAND

As someone who has had to empty many a waterlogged pot that has sat in its own juices for months on end, I can tell you it is not a fun job! The issue is also easily avoided by adding a little bit of sand or a few scoops of gravel. Neither material will harm your plants, and including it could pay dividends in the future. For plants that need a lot of drainage, such as bulbs – in particular lilies – and Mediterranean plants such as *Pelargoniums*, thyme or lavender, I would make the compost and gravel/sand mix a 50:50 split. The compost retains moisture and nutrients and gives the plant's roots a good structure to hold on to, while the sand or gravel allows the free movement of water around the roots and stops waterlogging. For less drought-tolerant species I would add a few scoopfuls of gravel or sand, just to help your plants out. If you have a bog pot or pond, then keep the gravel to a minimum. Succulents and cacti can be grown in gravel with just a little compost added.

WATER RETAINERS

The next additive that you can use is something that helps containers hold on to their moisture. Water-retaining additives come in all shapes and sizes. You can get some that are like clear glass marbles made out of jelly which slowly release their moisture and then shrink, or there are water-retaining crystals which look like crystalline salts and swell when you water your containers, slowly releasing their liquid over a period of time, meaning you need to water less frequently. They are really good for hanging baskets or pots that are hard to get to, or for adding to your pots if you are going away on a short trip. The easiest way to use these little beads of moisture is to add them to the compost as you are making up your containers. That way you won't cause any root damage by digging into the pot later, when the plants have established themselves.

PERLITE
+ VERMICULITE

They may sound more like ways to kill Superman than things you use in your garden, but trust me, perlite and vermiculite are brilliant. Perlite is exploded volcanic rock – a bit like pumice, but heated to incredibly high temperatures. These little bits of rock are totally inert, meaning they contain no nutrients, but also nothing harmful. They hold moisture because of all the air that's been introduced to the rock in the heating process, but do little else. That is why perlite is so good for growing cuttings, because it allows the stems to root without overfeeding, which can lead to weak growth. It is also really good to add to your compost because it increases drainage and adds moisture retention.

Perlite is also astoundingly light, making it a great addition or alternative to gravel or sand in a hanging basket or window box that you do not want to be too heavy for structural reasons. It is completely natural so it does not compromise any organic principles you might have – although there is a little energy required to heat the rock in the first place and also a few air miles associated with its import – and is a relatively cheap, easy and effective way of improving your compost. Try a 50:50 mix with a multi-purpose compost for general use in a container, and with seed and cutting compost for seeds and cuttings. Otherwise, try a 50:25:25 mix with half compost, a quarter gravel or sand and a quarter perlite. If the plants that you are growing are particularly moisture loving, don't overdo the perlite.

Vermiculite is a similar product to perlite and is used in a similar way. It is incredibly light and holds on to moisture, but also contains air, so it allows some gas exchange in the soil. It is made from hydrated minerals and because it is so light it is often used to top-dress the soil, particularly in seed containers, covering the seed with a light layer of moisture-retentive particles. It hasn't got the same structural integrity as perlite, so it gets squashed down into much smaller particles and breaks down quite quickly in the soil. That is not a bad thing, just different from the tenacious perlite. Essentially both perlite and vermiculite will do the same job, but one will do it for longer than the other.

FERTILISERS

You will need to add fertiliser to your containers throughout their lifetime. The easiest time to add fertiliser is when you are first planting up your pots, because that is the most effective way of dispersing it nice and evenly through the soil. This way the roots – both existing and potential new ones – will be fertilised in equal measure. So mix the fertiliser with the soil or compost, along with your gravel or perlite or sand – or all three – and your leaf mould and water-retaining crystals, then put it in your container along with your plant or plants. Simple(ish)!

NUTRIENTS

But what fertiliser do you use? There are 12 essential plant nutrients that will nearly all be present in whatever fertiliser you add to the soil, as well as in smaller quantities in the soil itself and the compost. These nutrients are:

Nitrogen
Phosphorus
Potassium
Sulphur
Magnesium
Calcium
Iron
Boron
Manganese
Zinc
Molybdenum
Copper

Of these 12 compounds, there are three that plants need in considerably higher quantities than the rest, and these will be represented on the packaging of whatever you buy in the form of a ratio. The nutrients are usually recorded in the following order: N (nitrogen): P (phosphates): K (potassium). These are known as primary nutrients. The rest of the compounds will not be shown on fertiliser packaging as they are needed in such miniscule quantities.

So what do those three major nutrients do? Well, **nitrogen** is needed by the leaves of the plant. If you are growing a shrub or an herbaceous plant that is grown more for its leaves than for its flowers, or a leafy vegetable, choose a fertiliser with a higher level of N. If you are using natural fertilisers this will be a substance like manure – chicken manure in particular is noted for its high nitrogen levels.

Phosphates are needed by roots; so any plant that may have a weak root system that must be built up, or one that has tubers, rhizomes or any kind of storage root, such as dahlias or root vegetables like carrots, will need higher levels of phosphates.

Potassium is required by the reproductive parts of a plant – the flowers and the fruits. For any plant that's grown solely for its fruits or for its flowers, use a fertiliser with a high level of potassium. For a natural version, seaweed, wood fire ash and bat manure are particularly good.

A word of warning: all plants need all these nutrients, plus many more, and nearly all fertilisers are higher in nitrogen than any other element. That is OK; don't be put off buying a fertiliser because it is high in nitrogen when you need something with high potassium, for example. Just look for the product that has the highest potassium level while bearing in mind it will still have more nitrogen than anything else.

TYPES OF FERTILISER

There are all kinds of fertilisers on the market, but they are all divided into two distinct groups: slow release and quick release. A slow-release fertiliser stays in the container for a number of weeks or months and seeps its nutrients slowly into the growing medium, providing a sustained feeding system. A quick-release fertiliser is, as the name suggests, an immediate and fleeting rush of nutrients. It gives a boost when it's needed and then is gone only days later. Both can be natural or synthetic, and organic or inorganic. I tend to stick to the organic kinds wherever possible. These usually take the form of manure (either horse – which is easiest to come by – cow or chicken), and these need six months to a year to season before they can be mixed straight into your compost. Essentially, this just means you leave the manure outside, usually undercover but not always, until the toxic compounds like ammonia have broken down to be replaced with usable compounds, like nitrates.

Another organic fertiliser is bonemeal – dried fish, blood and bone. This is a granular fertiliser that can be mixed up with the soil or scattered immediately around the roots of plants. It is technically a quick-release fertiliser, rapidly dissolved and absorbed, but it does also hang around in the soil for a few weeks, if not months.

It is worth noting at this point that the more free draining your soil, the quicker the fertiliser you add to it will be washed away. So there is a balance to be struck. For the perfect combination, you are aiming for a soil that is free draining, but (and this is the crucial bit) moisture retentive, unless your plant has specialised requirements.

Finally, a super quick-release fertiliser, and one that I use a lot, is comfrey tea. It is free to make if you have comfrey growing in your garden or it can be foraged with the landowner's permission. It is worth growing a pot of comfrey just to guarantee a constant supply of this precious liquid! (See right.) It works rather like tomato feed or liquid seaweed, and is added to your watering can.

For comfrey growers who want longer-lasting results, cut the leaves and dig them into or lay them on top of the soil. This makes a slow-release version of comfrey tea.

These are all organic options, but if you go to a garden centre you will also be able to find inorganic versions of all the above. Slow-release fertilisers usually come in pellet form and release their goodness into the soil over two to three months.

Although it can be tempting to pile it on when applying fertiliser, always read the instructions on the packet and err on the side of caution. Over-feeding plants, far from saving you time, can actually cause damage, by either stunting them badly or in the worst case killing them altogether. More is not always more when it comes to fertiliser, and a healthy balance is best.

COMFREY TEA RECIPE

To make comfrey tea, remove the leaves from the comfrey plant and immerse them in a bucket of water, stirring the concoction every few days for two months – you might want to pop a large stone on top to keep the leaves submerged. Do beware of the smell – it is potent. It's a good idea to cover the bucket with a lid and perhaps place it in a less-used part of your garden! After two months the comfrey tea can be diluted into your watering can at a ratio of one part comfrey tea to 10 parts water, then used to spot feed plants.

ALTERNATIVE MANURES

There are many other manures available, but they can be more difficult to get your hands on. Bat manure is incredibly high in potassium, so if you know a bat conservation society or anyone who has bat boxes it may be worth befriending them. Alpaca manure is also highly sought after – there are alpaca farms springing up all over the place and the manure is ripe for the picking. The great thing about alpaca manure is that it doesn't need to season at all – it can go straight from posterior to pot, so to speak. Just make sure you wear gloves when you handle it!

MULCH

Mulching is one of the last jobs you need to do when planting containers, and is optional but worth doing. A mulch can be a strange concept for non-gardeners; it is basically a layer of material that lies on the top of the soil, but it serves a good purpose.

It is designed to make your life easier and is surprisingly effective. It keeps the weeds at bay by preventing light getting to the soil, stopping them gaining strength. It also stops your containers losing too much water, which saves you watering regularly. Plus, it looks much more attractive than bare soil.

You don't *need* to add a mulch – the plants will not die without one – but when growing in containers that you want to be aesthetically pleasing, it does really help finish them off.

Gravel usually provides the nicest look, but you can also use bark, matting or even compost, which will feed the plants over time, too.

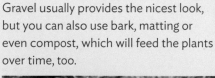

DRIP TRAY

Once your container is finished, with all the trimmings such as drainage, fertiliser, mulch and the plant itself in place, all that's left to do is water it. And here's where a drip tray comes in really handy.

A drip tray is a container that catches any excess water that runs through the soil and out of the pot's drainage holes, and there are a few good reasons for using them. The first is to prevent ruining any surfaces your container is perched on – your decking, balcony, windowsill or paving – by stopping water sitting around the base of your containers for long periods. Having a drip tray will also save you watering as frequently, because any water that flows right through the compost in the container will sit in the drip tray and get slowly pulled back up by the plant's roots through capillary action – the roots suck up the water like a straw. This has obvious benefits for the environment, too, as this means less water is wasted. However, do be careful not to over-water your plants; in general, plants do not like to sit in moisture all the time, so make sure your drip trays aren't always full of water.

As well as being really practical, drip trays can also be attractive. Often they may sit at the base of the pot and are pretty innocuous, but there are trays that entirely cover your pots, meaning you can pot plants into any old cheap container, then hide them entirely with a lovely, ornate drip tray.

Handy and practical – that's a combination that should never be sniffed at!

If your pot is very big and you don't want to ruin the floor, or if you have a very ornate floor and are worried the pot itself will cause damage, then placing your pot on a structure that will lift it off the ground can be a good idea.

PROJECTS

Whether you go to your local garden centre or an independent homeware shop, you will find that although there is a wide range of containers ready to buy, the truly inspiring ideas are often bespoke and can come with a hefty price tag. However, there is no reason why you cannot create your own personalised containers or use the containers that are on offer in a clever way to fit snugly into your garden. From pottery to pallets, there are cheap and easy ways of making any size or shape of container, and also new, decorative ways to display pots.

Remember in one container, plants will all get the same conditions. I have created projects that will grow well together. They can easily be adapted but always make sure that if you're planting more than one species together, they all need to require the same growing conditions.

1

HOT-COLOURED DISPLAYS ON A LADDER

🕐 **AN AFTERNOON**

An old wooden stepladder makes a great prop and a brilliant space-saving device to show off your most prized potted plants. A rustic old set of steps is most exciting when offset by the striking use of a modern colour palette of plants. I have used hot colours to make this feel a little more tropical and edgy, but it would work equally well with a full cottage-garden feel and pastel colours. You could paint the ladder with neutral or dark colours like navy to offset the hot palette planting, but for added heat, try a lick of a bold paint – royal blue, bright red or orange. Or, if you have the space (and the ladders), all three together could look fantastic when crammed with plants! Or just paint the pots!

YOU WILL NEED

An old wooden stepladder
Exterior multisurface paint in
    your favourite colour
    (optional)
Brackets and bolts for fixing the
    ladder to the wall or floor
Lots of terracotta pots – differing
    sizes are fine
Compost
A delicious mix of hot-coloured
    plants and tempering plants
Try a second set of display pots
    for the winter months,
    focusing more on foliage
    and evergreen species such as
    evergreen ferns, *Ruscus,
    Skimmia, Vinca, Phormium,*
    conifer species or evergreen
    grasses

METHOD

1. If painting the ladder, do that first.
2. Place the ladder where you intend to display it. The plants should be the main focus, so think about the backdrop carefully. A neutral wall will enhance the floral display. Also think about the ladder's placement in practical terms; you don't want to be tripping over it and creating a terracotta tumble, so put it where it can be easily seen, but doesn't interfere with any activities.
3. Attach it to either the wall or to the floor in order to ensure it stays securely in place. Use brackets that attach to the ladder and the wall or floor and bolt into place securely.
4. Half-fill the pots with compost then add the hot-coloured and tempering plants of purple or silver – the more pots, the more impact your display will have. For a modern feel, keep pots to a neat minimum – choose a certain number per shelf and stick to it. Three works well, as odd numbers always look more pleasing.
5. Arrange the pots so that the tallest plants are not impinging too much on the plants above. Make sure the colour arrangement is balanced, with bright colours evenly spread out. The plants on the top rungs will probably get more intense sunlight than the those on the lower rungs.
6. Water regularly. Feed flowering or even fruiting plants such as *Pelargoniums,* tomatoes, chillies, marigolds, *Rudbeckia* and *Dahlias* throughout the season with a high-potash liquid feed.

**A gorgeous mix of
hot-coloured plants**
Red hot pokers
Verbena
Pelargoniums
Begonia
Rudbeckias
Zinnia
Gazania
Crocosmia
Dahlias
Helenium
Elymus
Salvia
Lobelia cardinalis
Papaver
Hedera helix 'Goldheart'
Thunbergia alata
   (these last two are
   great for cascades)
Echinacea

Tempering plants
Hot colours can be a bit
much unless tempered
with something that
offers a relief for the
eye. Try:
Purple sage
Allium
Senecio cineraria
Melianthus major
Purple cabbage
Lavender
Salvia nemorosa
Perovskia
Eryngium
Artemisia

2

OLD PALLET WITH OLIVE TREES

 AN AFTERNOON

Be careful when selecting your pallets – the blocks that separate the two frames are sometimes made of solid wood and other times of reconstituted wood pulp. Some are already broken, others not, and some have tops with no gaps, which means there's more good wood to be used.

Also remember that pallet wood is never tanalised, so you will need to either treat it yourself or think carefully about what you plant in it – never plant anything that requires lots of water, and place the container somewhere that avoids a lot of rainfall. This is why I have chosen an olive tree to plant in this container; it can cope with full sun, some wind and needs very little water. Perfect for a pallet.

YOU WILL NEED

Protective clothing, including
 gloves and goggles
Shovel/crowbar
A pallet or two (You will need
 to cover the sides of a box at least
 30cm cubed. You can cut the
 wood off the framework of your
 pallets or you can lever them off
 and cut them to size, in which
 case you will need fewer pallets.)
Saw
Hammer
Screws and screwdriver
Staple gun
Permeable membrane or liner
Washed horticultural grit/gravel
Multi-purpose compost
Olive tree
Slate chippings
Gravel mulch (optional)

METHOD

1. Using your shovel, prise the pallet wood apart until you have separated the planks from the supporting framework. This can be a tricky process; for it to work best put your pallet on a stable surface. If you find that this is too tough and the wood splits before it comes off the pallet, cut the wood off its framework, but be aware that this will give you much shorter planks.
2. Hammer any nails out of the timber so that it is safe to handle.
3. Construct a cube from the thicker supporting timber originally used for the frame of the pallet. The cube must be big enough to hold the root ball of your tree and preferably at least a third bigger to give the roots room to grow (usually at least 30cm cubed).
4. Cut the pallet planks to a length that's just above the height of your cube, then screw these to the cube you've made – they can be horizontal or vertical, depending on your personal preference.
5. Screw the pallet planks to the underside of your cube, making sure you leave gaps between them for any water to escape through.
6. Turn the cube the right way up, then, using a staple gun, attach the liner to the inside of the container.
7. Mix the grit or gravel with the compost in either a 50:50 mix or with slightly more gravel than compost.
8. Put a few inches of gritty compost in the bottom of the container. Place your olive tree in the container and fill all the gaps around it with the remaining compost. Water well, then top the container with slate chippings.

13 GREAT ALTERNATIVES TO AN OLIVE

Rock rose
Chaenomeles speciosa
Nandina domestica
Abelia x grandiflora
Olearia macrodonta
Elaeagnus ebbingei
Eucalyptus gunnii
Koelreuteria paniculata
Cercis siliquastrum
Callistemon citrinus
Acacia dealbata
Melianthus major
Sorbus aria

3

A PRAIRIE-INSPIRED, UPCYCLED METAL BIN

AN HOUR

The prairie style is a contemporary planting scheme that has become popular in the last few decades. It uses a lot of greens, particularly grasses, but offsets them with flowers that are naturally found in prairies and savannahs. As well as being stylish, it is also a very low-maintenance scheme which will cope with most conditions. So really it is win-win, especially when combined with a tasteful container. Some grasses are also evergreen, providing year-round interest, which is always a bonus.

For this project I am using metal as a contemporary material to pair with the planting, though you could use any type of container. When using metal it is important to put a membrane between the container and the soil to prevent the plants' roots overheating and scorching, as metal gets very hot.

TIP... Add bulbs for year-round interest.

For an alternative use *Eupatorium rugosum* 'Chocolate' and *Panicum virgatum* 'Heavy Metal'.

I've used:
Grasses *Carex morrowii* (variegated) and *Miscanthus sinensis*
Flowers Chocolate cosmos (*Cosmos atrosanguineus*), but any plant with a traditional daisy-like flower will give a prairie feel.

PRAIRIE PLANTER IDEAS

Annual prairie – Annual poppy with *Panicum elegans* and *Cosmos*.

Purple and yellow prairie – *Stipa gigantea*, *Echinacea*, *Verbena bonariensis* and *Stipa tenuissima*.

Daisy flower prairie – *Echinacea purpurea*, *Rudbeckia*, *Briza media* and *Stipa tenuissima*. In a shady spot *Anemone x hybrida* can replace other flowers.

YOU WILL NEED

An upcycled box big enough for at
    least 10 plants
A drill with a metal drill bit
Some plastic or impermeable liner,
    thickish for maximum insulation – or
    use bubble wrap with holes cut in for
    drainage
Crocks, horticultural grit or small stones
Compost – most soil types will do,
    depending on your plant species, but
    a multi-purpose compost mixed with
    topsoil is fine for most species
Sand
Grasses of your choice
Flowering plants of your choice

METHOD

1. Drill at least five good-sized (2cm diameter) holes in the bottom of your container for drainage.
2. Spread the liner inside the container for insulation – you don't need to attach it (metal is very hard to attach anything to), the compost will hold it in place once the container is filled. If you prefer, you can apply masking tape to the liner until the compost is in place.
3. Make five big holes in the liner, corresponding with those you've drilled into the bottom of the pot, to allow water to drain away.
4. Place plenty of crocks in the bottom of the container – they don't have to cover the whole base but the more you have the less chance there is of your container waterlogging. If you don't have enough broken pots, some horticultural grit or small stones will do the job.
5. Mix the compost with some sand – a few scoops or shovels full will do.
6. Fill the container with your compost mix, two thirds of the way up.
7. Arrange the grasses and flowers in the container – how you do this depends on where you put the container (see opposite). Play with the planting arrangement until you are happy – you can always move plants around later if you change your mind.
8. Fill any gaps around the plants' root balls with the remaining compost, then water them in well.
9. Feed the plants a little throughout the growing season with some slow-release fertilisers, but try not to overdo it – perennials don't need as much food as annual plants.

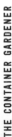

ARRANGING PLANTS IN A CONTAINER

If the container will be viewed from all directions, you may want to put the tallest plants in the centre, but concealing plants behind taller plants so that they're only seen from certain angles can be effective, especially in modern schemes. If your container will be set against a wall, put the tallest plants at the back so that all of them are shown off to their full potential. You could also cascade everything down from one corner. In a lot of prairie planting, the plants are arranged in a linear style, which is a nice option – just put all the plants of any one species in a line together.

UPCYCLED
WORK BOOTS

🕐 **1 HOUR**

The great thing about outdoor work boots is that they are so large. But what do you do when you are finished with them? They are not fit for purpose and unsafe once they get old and worn through, but with all that wasted space, they really lend themselves to being turned into containers.

This project should be planted in the spring so that your bedding plants have time to produce the best displays. When choosing your plants, simply pick your favourite colours. The varieties I have used (see opposite) are easy to get hold of, come in a huge range of colours and you can change the display every year. If you are not a fan of annuals then grow perennials instead, just feed the pots every year and change the compost every couple of years. These containers are incredibly versatile; you can swap out the plants and easily move around the lightweight containers to maximise their impact throughout the season.

YOU WILL NEED

An old pair of work boots –
   or even a few pairs
Drill (optional)
Crocks
Multi-purpose compost
Slow-release fertiliser or granular fertiliser
Dibber (optional)
Annual bedding of your choice –
   in plugs in the spring is best. I used marigolds, *Petunias*, *Senecio cineraria*, *Tagetes*, *Begonias* and *Pelargonium*

METHOD

1. Make sure there are holes in the bottom of your old boots – if they don't already have them from over-use, drill a few into the rubber sole, being careful of any steel midsoles they may have.
2. Place a few pieces of crocks in the bottom of the boots for drainage.
3. Fill the boots with compost mixed with a little fertiliser. Using a dibber or your finger, make holes in the compost and place a plug plant in each hole. Firm the soil around each plant.
4. Water the finished boots and feed every two weeks with a liquid fertiliser, such as tomato feed, seaweed feed or comfrey tea (page 57). After the bedding has gone over, collect their seeds for next year (on a dry day) and compost the plant material.
5. They will flourish in almost any position, as long as they get some sun and plenty of food and water. Bedding plants really want to flower so will cope with most positions. Do protect them from very high winds, though, as these can snap the tender stems.

I have used a variety of shades for a bright display, including classics like *Petunia, Senecio cineraria, Tagetes* and *Begonias*.

5

A WILDLIFE GARDEN IN AN UPCYCLED SUITCASE

 1 HOUR

The best way to create a natural ecosystem in your garden is to make it a haven not only for you, but for the local wildlife, too. Butterflies and bees make a garden feel like a secluded patch of wilderness, and introducing wildlife is also a brilliant way to get kids enthused about the great outdoors. Incidentally, insect-friendly plants also tend to be the most floriferous and beautiful. What works for the bees works for us too.

For something a little different, and much cheaper, than a big container you could use an old suitcase. They can be easily found in charity shops or garage sales for a fraction of the price you would pay for a more traditional container of the same size. The suitcase will need to be able to withstand a bit of weather, so look for one made of wood or tough leather. It will break down a little over the course of a few years, but this will only add to its vintage look. You will be surprised how well leather wears – even in the great outdoors.

YOU WILL NEED

Old suitcase made from wood or tough leather, deep enough for a 3 -litre pot and wide enough for at least six plants

Drill (or Stanley knife or craft knife if you're using a leather case or if you don't have a drill)

Washed horticultural grit or gravel, plus gravel to mulch

Buddleja, Salvia, Sedum, lavender, borage, *Allium, Veronicastrum, Phlox,* mallow, *Hebe, Papaver,* foxgloves or *Campanula*

Compost – not too heavy, including bark or grit

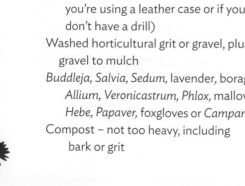

METHOD

1. Drill or cut holes in the bottom of the suitcase to create drainage. Generally speaking, the more the merrier, as these plants require a fairly free-draining soil, but you need at least five good-sized holes.

2. Place the suitcase in its final position. If you have a small suitcase you can move it after planting, but generally, especially with a large container, it is better to plant it in situ.

3. Add a 2.5–5cm-deep layer of washed horticultural grit or gravel to the bottom of the suitcase and cover with a few inches of compost. This should form a layer on which you can place the plants so that the top of their root balls come to about 2.5cm from the rim. This way you avoid burying your plants too deeply.

4. Place the plants in the suitcase in a pleasing arrangement. The *Buddleja* and *Salvia* (or any other taller plants) should go at the back of your arrangement so that they do not block the light for the other plants. The *Sedum* will be lovely at the front where it can tumble over the edge of the case.

5. Once you are happy, backfill with more compost until the soil level is just below the rim of the suitcase.

6. Dress the compost with a layer of gravel to finish off.

7. Water the container well so that all the roots are guaranteed to make good contact with the soil.

8. Cut the *Buddleja* back in the early spring so that it can put on nice growth through the season. Cut lavender in spring but do not go into the woody stems. The other plants will need cutting back in the autumn and protecting from the worst of the frost. Every year give a light feed of compost and top off with a mulch, then every three to four years, repot and replace the compost completely.

TIP... This particular arrangement does best placed in the sun or part shade, as all of these plants require some sunlight. It is also a great way of making sure the insects see it!

6

A WINDOWSILL HERB GARDEN IN A DISPLAY CRATE

🕐 **1 HOUR**

From a gardener's perspective, herbs are a delight to grow. They need hardly any water, feeding or root space, which means you can grow them in the smallest spaces with relative success. For the best plants to get started with, go to a garden centre or grow them from seed – especially basil, nothing ever tastes as good as basil grown from seed. Herbs in a garden centre are grown for growing on rather than for instant eating, so I would recommend them over anything you buy from the supermarket.

Another great thing about growing herbs in one pot, particularly if you stick to Mediterranean herbs, such as oregano, thyme, rosemary, sage and marjoram, which all like dry, free-draining soil (with some moisture) and full sunlight, is that it avoids the pitfall of growing things together that actually don't like the same conditions, leading to some dying and others thriving over time.

These kinds of herbs don't need much space for their roots as they grow wild on rocky ground, so you can squeeze this little container onto a windowsill or the smallest patio.

TIP... Put this crate somewhere that's easily accessible when you're cooking or eating. Making this the centrepiece on your outdoor table is really effective, as it releases its herby scents while you're eating al fresco and is also handy to pick at, too.

YOU WILL NEED

Old wooden crate, that will fit on a windowsill or in the middle of a table
Drill and 1cm drill bit
Multi-purpose compost
Grit
Herbs of your choice

METHOD

1. Make some holes in the base of your container – herbs need plenty of drainage so drill at least two holes for each plant, each at least 1cm in diameter. The more holes the better, without upsetting the stability of the pot.
2. Mix the compost with the grit in a ratio of about 50:50 and add most of it to the container.
3. Arrange your herbs in the container, making sure the colours and textures are evenly spread out – so that not all the purples in one area and not all the strappy foliage in another. Spread similar-looking plants around to create a balanced arrangement.
4. Fill any spaces around the plants with the remaining compost, then water the plants well.
5. This container is low maintenance, though you might find that as you use the herbs they will become depleted of foliage and in time you might want to replace any herbs that look a bit raggedy. Most Mediterranean herbs need minimal water and food, with the exception of basil and coriander, which both need a little more water.

I've used thyme,
rosemary, sage,
chives and golden
marjoram.

7

BOG GARDEN IN A BUTLER SINK

🕐 **1 HOUR**

Butler sinks are beautiful. So much so that even when sold second-hand, they still cost a fair bit. As an addition to the garden, they are fantastic – clean, crisp and white, so they look modern, but they are also rustic and sturdy enough to have gravitas and class. They lend themselves best to one of two options – a pond or a bog garden. This is because they have very limited drainage capabilities, unless you drill more holes into the base, which would cause their value to depreciate. Turning a butler sink into a bog garden is very simple and adds a touch of mystery to something that is effortlessly stylish.

YOU WILL NEED

Compost

Water-retaining crystals or beads

Butler sink or other non-permeable container – it could be a metal trough or bin or even a big bowl. You will need very few drainage holes – one small one to get rid of the worst of the moisture should be enough

Plants – any of those on the right though remember that a butler sink is not huge, so stick to three plants maximum. For a modern effect stick to a single species:

Ligularia dentata
'Othello' or *Ligularia amplexicaulis* **'Britt Marie Crawford'**
Rodgersia
Persicaria
Myosotis scopiodes
Rheum palmatum
Gunnera magellanica
Gunnera manicata
Eupatorium
Iris laevigata
Trollius
Geum rivale
Primula japonica
Grasses
Juncus effusus
Carex elata
Ferns
Osmunda regalis
Matteuccia
Athyrium filix-femina
Equisetum

METHOD

1. Mix the compost with water-retaining crystals or beads according to the instructions on the packet.

2. Fill the sink with the compost mix, covering the plug hold with gravel or crockery to allow for drainage and to prevent toxic build-up of anaerobic conditions (see opposite).

3. Plant your plants into the compost and water them in.

4. Make sure the plants never dry out by regularly feeling the soil to check if it is moist. If you see any sign of the leaves wilting or becoming curled or crispy, give the pot a good water. Equally though, these are not marginals, so do not leave them sitting in constant water. Nicely damp is perfect.

5. Cut plants back to the crown (right in the centre of the plants) once they have died down, or to a few inches above soil level.

6. Protect the crowns of plants from extreme cold by covering them with horticultural fleece or straw, as often bog plants don't like to be too cold. *Gunnera* can be protected with its own leaves, but note that if you are using *Gunnera* it has now been classified as an invasive plant so should not be planted anywhere near flowing water.

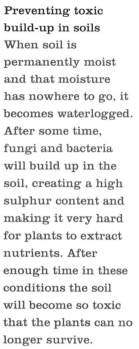

Preventing toxic build-up in soils
When soil is permanently moist and that moisture has nowhere to go, it becomes waterlogged. After some time, fungi and bacteria will build up in the soil, creating a high sulphur content and making it very hard for plants to extract nutrients. After enough time in these conditions the soil will become so toxic that the plants can no longer survive.

8

A PALLET LIVING WALL

 AN AFTERNOON

Pallets are our modern answer to nearly every design conundrum. As I mentioned in project two, the most arduous part about using a pallet is prising the planks apart and painstakingly removing every nail. So in this project, there is no need for that, you can use the pallet as it is. Just make sure you pick one that looks nice, with no split timbers or bits hanging off it.

One consideration for a living wall is that it can cause damp, so it's a good idea to add a plastic backing to your living wall and prepare the wall before you install your feature – a waterproof, exterior PVA paint does the job, or a specialist, damp-proof masonry paint. Also, the weight of a watered, plant-filled pallet is quite considerable, so a single-skin wall that goes into your property isn't suitable for this project, nor a dry stone or crumbly wall. I would strongly recommend that if you have any doubts, get a professional to look at the wall you are planning to use before you go ahead.

Lastly, when choosing the position of your living wall, try to avoid a wall that is fully south-facing or north-facing as these positions create challenging conditions for the plants, either getting far too hot or far too damp and cold. An easterly/south-easterly or a westerly/south-westerly position is infinitely better.

YOU WILL NEED

Water-permeable liner
An old pallet (or other green wall device)
Staple gun or clout nails and hammer
Sheet of strong plastic
Drill with masonry bit and screwdriver attachment
Rawlplugs
Screws
Compost
Water-retaining crystals
Plants – preferably including some cascading varieties but you can choose what you like

Small rooting species such as strawberries, lettuce, *Galium*, *Alchemilla*, ferns, succulents and alpines (mountain plants like *Saxifraga*) work best. For practical gardeners this is a great opportunity to grow some herbs, vegetables (most annual veg will survive in semi-stressed conditions though they may be more prone to bolting if you are growing leafy veg), so tomatoes, chillies, lettuce, purple sprouting broccoli, sprouts, strawberries, etc. For the ornamental-lovers, use plants like lavender, rosemary (especially the prostrate form), ivy, *Sedums* and other succulents, *Lobelia* (cascading) *Erigeron*, etc. It can be a great idea to colour theme your green wall so that it's not-so-green – purple is a really effective choice, as there are plenty of purple edibles and ornamentals that grow well in limited space (see page 98).

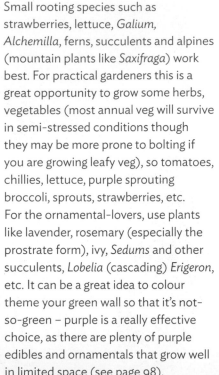

If you like the linear element of a pallet you can also make a living wall using the verticals rather than the horizontals. Line the whole pallet interior leaving a gap at the top. Fill with compost, plant in the gaps and then leave it flat on the floor until the roots hold the soil in place, otherwise you will find things tend to fall out. This version will be much heavier and harder to fit to the wall, though, so you may need assistance.

METHOD

1. Attach the liner behind each horizontal plank of your pallet in using the staple gun or clout nails – double it up if you want to ensure that it is extra strong. The depth of a pallet plank should be enough to house a plant. The pockets should be deep enough to accommodate the entire root ball of the plants. Ideally the pockets should be no lower than the plant of the pallet, meaning that you will probably need to buy plants that are in 9cm pots or smaller.

2. Fix the strong plastic to the back of the whole pallet with a staple gun or clout nails, to protect your walls from damp.

3. Drill at least six holes into the wall (two at the bottom, two at the top and two in the middle) – the more attachment points there are, the stronger it will be. If you are worried about this you can lean your pallet wall at an angle against the wall. It does not actually have to be attached. Insert the rawlplugs.

4. Screw your pallet to the wall using screws that go into each rawlplug (make sure you have enough for a really strong fitting).

5. Mix your compost with the water-retaining crystals following the instructions on the packet.

6. Fill each pocket with compost mix. Along each channel of compost, plant your plants, ensuring there is room for each of them to grow.

7. If you add a cascading plant every few plants, and stagger them as you move up the height of the pallet, within a few months the whole pallet will be engulfed by plants. This looks much nicer than neat lines.

9

OLD COLANDER HANGING BASKET

 1 HOUR

You can make a hanging basket out of a colander, bird cage, wok, cheese grater or indeed anything old and metal that can be hung up. These 'junk' items make brilliant containers when they've served their usefulness. A colander in particular, with its pre-drilled holes, can become a beautiful hanging basket, as it is very free draining, so ideal for growing plants that can cope with dry conditions, such as Mediterranean herbs, ivy, succulents, *Pelargoniums* and other sun-lovers. You could also use annual bedding, bought and planted as plugs in the spring, for a brighter, more traditional look.

YOU WILL NEED

Water-permeable liner
Scissors
An old metal or plastic colander
Strong rope or chains
Hooks that are fairly strong – they
    need to safely hold a heavy
    container complete with plants
    and water (heavy-duty hooks or
    hanging basket brackets can be
    bought from a garden centre or
    online)
Water-retaining crystals
Slow-release fertiliser, such as
    chicken manure pellets or
    granular feed
Compost
Plants to fill it, such as Mediterranean
    herbs, ivy, succulents,
    Pelargoniums. I've used:
    margerites, *Senecio cineraria*,
    bronze fennel and ivy

Cascading species, such as trailing *Pelargoniums*, ivy, *Aubretia*, *Lobelia*, *Lampranthus*, *Sedum* or *Erigeron* are great in a hanging basket that's high up, as they bring the flowers or foliage down to eye level, which means you're not looking at the base of your pot instead of the plants themselves.

METHOD

1. Cut the liner so that it fits in the colander exactly and fit the rope or chains to it.

2. Screw the hooks into the ceiling or wall, or whatever you're hanging your colander from – one per hanging basket. Make sure they are well attached and heavy duty enough to hold the weight of the colander plus plants, compost and, crucially, water (always the heaviest component of a planter).

3. Mix the compost with the water-retaining crystals and fertiliser following the instructions on the packet.

4. Place a little compost in the bottom of the colander, then arrange your plants – remember that unless the basket is in the centre of the garden or right in front of a window, you might only ever see it from three sides, so make sure your design takes this into account.

5. Backfill any gaps around the roots of the plants with the remaining compost, hang the colander from the hook and water it well. It is always best to do this when it's in situ as the weight of the hanging basket will be considerably greater, making it harder to hang once it's watered.

6. Feed throughout the summer with a slow-release fertiliser and liquid feed added to the water when an extra boost is needed.

10

RAISED BED MADE FROM RAILWAY SLEEPERS

🕐 **A WEEKEND**

Raised beds are a great way to grow, and depending on their size, you can grow a really wide range of species. Railway sleepers are ideal for raised beds, but they are literally not to be taken lightly! If you have a bad back, you may want to get some help with this project. But the great thing about sleepers is that once they are in place, they are heavy enough that they almost don't need supporting, just fixing together at the corners.

This is a big project but well worth the effort for the amount of growing space it provides – and they look great; modern but naturalistic. You can make these beds sleek or a little rough around the edges, depending on how geometric you make your design. I have gone for two rectangles; one filled with vegetables, one with wild flowers. This is partly for ease, as sleepers are a set length. I ordered mine from a timber merchant at either full lengths or ready-cut half-lengths. Cutting these is a professional job, so unless you are fully trained, I'd leave it to the professionals.

YOU WILL NEED

Spade

Gloves, goggles and steel-toe-cap boots

3, 6 or 9 tanalised railway sleepers, depending how tall you want your raised bed

4 wood battens (5 x 5cm or 7.5 x 7.5cm)

Drill and 2.5cm wood drill bit

Screwdriver

Long screws or bolts – 2 per sleeper

Dowel – 2.5cm diameter

Wood glue

Mallet

Staple gun

Waterproof liner

Topsoil – about 2 cubic metres per sleeper rectangle

Compost – you will often find green waste compost from the local council, delivered in large quantity, or you can make it yourself (see page 53)

Well-rotted manure (for vegetables only)

Plants to fill it – wildflower plug plants, such as poppies, cornflowers and yarrow, or vegetable plugs such as kale, cabbage, lettuce, climbing French beans, sweetcorn, tomatoes, beetroots, celeriac, etc. I'd stick to half the bed for one plant family and the other half for another to allow easy crop rotation (see page 157)

TIP... You can often get topsoil delivered from local housing developments where they are clearing a lot of it to build foundations. And if you have already made your beds they could even drop it straight in for you, saving hours of barrowing.

METHOD

1. Choose where you want the bed to go – once built a raised bed is almost impossible to move. Level the ground – any uneven surfaces will make your structure less sturdy and potentially wobbly. The easiest way to do this is to dig out using a spade, but don't dig down too deeply. If there is a real slope you may want to create some proper terracing. The finished result should be a strong, firm surface that can hold the weight of a raised bed. You can create a level base with a concrete foundation, but this will narrow your planting options, as the plants' roots won't be able to go deeper than the depth of the bed.

2. Lay out your sleepers – you may want to enlist some help with this as they are pretty heavy – preferably wearing protective kit.

3. With someone holding the sleepers in place, screw the battens of wood to the inside corners using some hefty bolts or screws. You should have at least two screws per sleeper on each side of the batten so that the corner is held securely. This will stop the sleepers moving when you finally attach them and give extra support when they're finished.

4. Drill two holes (about 3cm) into the uncut end of each outer corner with the drill bit.

5. Drill a pilot hole into the wood starting from inside this 2.5cm hole.

6. Screw in the heavy duty bolts so that they sit tight with the surface at the back of the 2.5cm hole and make sure they go well into the attaching sleeper.

7. Cut a 3cm length of dowel and cover it with a layer of wood glue. Using the mallet, hammer it into the hole so that it sits flush against the sleeper or just proud of it, if you like a more rustic look.

8. Using the staple gun, attach the liner to the inside of the sleeper walls, but not along the ground, as this would prevent natural drainage.

9. Fill the beds with the compost, topsoil and manure – if you are growing vegetables. The majority of the blend should be topsoil, with a few inches depth of compost, and a few inches depth of manure. Fork it all so that it is nicely mixed.

10. Plant it up in the spring. Wild flowers need watering in and watering regularly. Vegetables need regular water and feeding with an organic fertiliser either in the form of a liquid feed like seaweed or comfrey tea, or as granular pellets such as bonemeal or chicken manure pellets.

11. In the autumn, cut back your wildflowers; once the seeds have formed scatter them on the ground for the following year. Keep a few aside to sow in spring and fill in any gaps.

12. Once you have harvested your vegetables, either grow a green manure in the bed over winter, or mulch with seasoned farmyard manure, ready for next year's crops.

GROWING VEG IN RAISED BEDS

In terms of vegetables, the world is your oyster, from brassicas like cabbage, lettuce and kale to peas and other legumes, as well as fruiting crops such as tomatoes and peppers, nasturtiums, sweetcorn (especially effective if planted as a hedge separating other plant families) and many more. The only thing you need to remember is that you must rotate the crops every year (see page 157). Also, you may struggle to grow potatoes because they need soil to be mounded up around their growing stems, so these are better in a standard container.

11

A HEDGE IN A POT

🕐 **1 HOUR**

You may not have an outdoor area that requires a huge beech hedge à la Louis XIV and his gardens at Versailles, but even in the humblest of spaces a little privacy goes a long way. Perhaps you want to eat outside without your neighbours judging your cookery skills, or you want to be more scantily clad in warm weather. Whatever your reasons for privacy, a hedge is a great way to achieve it. If you have a small plot, there is no reason not to plant that hedge in the ground, but if you really don't have much space, such as on a roof terrace, a balcony or a courtyard on which you are not allowed to break the paving, a potted hedge is a really good option. It can also be a useful method of division within your garden. Adding height always makes for a more interesting design, which plays tricks on the eye, so you could plant a hedge to divide your outdoor space and create private escapes in hidden corners, or to hide eyesores like trampolines and swings from the more adult areas of the garden. You could do this simply with a line of pots, too.

YOU WILL NEED

A trough or several similar-sized pots arranged in a line – an absolute minimum of three to achieve the desired effect

Hedging plants, such as beech, *Griselinia* for a coastal spot, hornbeam, box, yew, if you want evergreens, cherry laurel and bamboo, cherry for something productive, or, similarly, an espaliered apple for a flat, attractive and productive hedge, alder, hazel, something pleached for a higher or even a two-tier hedge. But anything will do, including lavender, rosemary and *Phormium*, especially in a tall pot

Topsoil or multi-purpose compost

Stakes for the hedging plants and string (optional)

METHOD

1. Place the trough or containers in position before you start planting so that you can make sure everything is in the right place, otherwise they will be heavy and difficult to move once planted up, particularly in the case of the trough.

2. Put a thin layer of topsoil or compost in the bottom of the container(s).

3. Lay out your hedging plants root ball to root ball, or so that the foliage knits together at the top and you cannot see through it. If you are using espalier apples or pleached specimens, leave a large gap between the root balls so that the edges of the branches just or almost touch.

4. Backfill around the plants and into any spaces with the remaining compost or topsoil. Firm down the soil with your hands.

5. You may want to attach a stake or frame for additional support if the area is exposed to wind – on a roof terrace or balcony, for example. Push a stake or cane into the soil and tie the hedge plant to it, using string. In severely windy spots, you may want to stake at a 45-degree angle into the prevailing wind, or attach your plants using string to a balustrade, fence or trellis.

6. Water well. Feed with a slow-release fertiliser once a year or mulch with compost in the winter.

7. Refresh the compost or repot every few years, or do so if the leaves begin to lose their lustre, the plants do not flower so vigorously, look a little cramped, or the leaves begin to discolour – all of which indicate a lack of nutrients.

TIP... It's best to make this project in autumn or winter when you can buy bare-root shrubs and trees for far less than container-grown ones will cost in the spring or summer.

12

NEVER THROW AWAY A TIN AGAIN!

⏱ 1 HOUR

There is a lot of visual worth and versatility in a tin. Andy Warhol recognised it and now gardeners are beginning to recognise it, too. Tins are great because they are so changeable. They start off with a lovely glossy label or decoration, which quickly ages and rusts or oxydises and begins to look decidedly arcadian. They come in varying sizes, too, and are usually filled with delicious food, so you have the best of both worlds – you can eat the contents then grow in the receptacle. And if you're food obsessed like me, you can grow more food in it, or herbs. Tins are also fairly lightweight compared with a lot of containers, which means you can arrange them more ingeniously – such as by screwing them to the wall or upright on a balcony or pergola.

YOU WILL NEED

Tins – as many as you have, a collection that can be added to as time goes on. They don't all have to be one size, the more varied the better!

Drill

Varnish and paintbrush

Screws, if you want to attach them to anything

Sand or gravel for drainage

Water-retaining crystals

Compost

Plants – anything small will lend itself to this as there will be limited root space. Strawberries, lettuces and herbs are the best edibles and succulents, annuals, mosses and alpines make the best ornamentals.

METHOD

1. Drill drainage holes in the bottom of your tins. One hole is OK if you use enough gravel, but I'd suggest three to be on the safe side (more for large tins).

2. Varnish the inside of the tin; a tin can is actually made from steel and coated with tin or, confusingly, with aluminium, so the coating will eventually wear away to expose the steel beneath. The tin and aluminium get into the soil and the rusting steel will do the same. This is not good for the plants, as increased heavy metals in the soil lead to a change in pH and affect plants' ability to soak up nutrients. These compounds in the soil are also very harmful to humans if eaten, so a layer of varnish is very important particularly if you are planning to grow edibles.

3. Wait for the varnish to dry – this will take 12–48 hours. If in doubt, wait for as long as possible; tacky varnish could mean the compost sticks to the tin, which would look dreadful and be hard to get off.

4. Using a drill, make a hole in the back of the tin then screw it onto a wall or post. The positioning of the tins dictates what you can grow; place alpines in a bright, exposed location, and mosses or ferns in a shady corner. If it's a dry spot, succulents are the order of the day.

5. Mix the sand or gravel, water-retaining crystals and compost together, making a 50:50 mix of sand or gravel and compost and adding the crystals according to the packet instructions. Add a layer of the mix to the bottom of the tin.

6. Place the plants in the tin. Backfill around the roots using the remaining compost mix until the pots are full. Water well.

7. Succulents need bringing in during a wet winter. Ferns may need a replenished compost every few years or a mulch of fresh compost every year. Cut off any dead, dying or diseased material as and when you see it.

13

SUCCULENT PICTURE FRAME

 **AN AFTERNOON**

As a gardener you have to do absolutely nothing in order to successfully grow succulents. They need minimal watering – in a temperate climate they're more likely to be killed off from excessive water than from drought. They need hardly any root space and they propagate with absolutely no effort at all (see the tip on page 95). This extraordinary talent for survival makes them incredibly versatile. You can grow succulents in the smallest of spaces (stuffed into a hollowed-out cork) or en masse in a huge area. They make great table centrepieces as they never get too tall and they look lovely cascading from any upcycled receptacle – a tea pot, tea tin, tiny pot or display of tiny pots, stuffed into the cracks on gnarled wood, etc.

There are the traditional rosette forms that have become so popular (in all colours, textures and sizes – hairy, fluffy, chalky white, green, purple, black, red, etc.), but these can be susceptible to damping off in the autumn and over winter. If you live somewhere with a colder, wetter climate, there are many traditional succulents that are more tolerant of a little rain and cold – such as sedums. For some people (myself included) who live by the sea, succulents like *Lampranthus* (or as people where I live affectionately know it, 'Pig face') are some of the only reliable plants that grow in the salty conditions.

For this project, I am making a picture frame to hang on the wall, crammed full of succulents. The finished article will fit into the smallest space, and with minimal water requirements, could even be complemented by some battery-powered or solar lighting for maximum effect.

YOU WILL NEED

An old picture frame with a deep recess
     of about 5cm
Thin plywood and fine batons
Screws
Drill
Chicken wire or mesh
Compost
Horticultural grit or sand
Dibber
Lots of succulents, some hanging like
     Sedum rupestre or *Sedum*
     spathulifolium, Crassula multicava
     and some rosettes like *Sempervivum*
     tectorum, S. arachnoideum (which
     means like spiderwebs), *S. calcareum,*
     Echeveria glauca, E. agavoides 'Black
     Prince' or *Sedum* x *rubrotinctum*

METHOD

1. If the picture frame has a glass front, remove the glass and dispose of it safely.
2. Make a box to fit on the back of the picture frame using the plywood screwed together with fine batons.
3. Where the glass would normally go, attach the chicken wire or mesh.
4. Fix the box to the back of the picture frame.
5. Drill holes for drainage in the bottom of the picture frame; you need lots of holes as succulents need very good drainage.
6. Mix the compost with plenty of grit or sand. Pour the compost into the picture- frame box.
7. Break off succulent plants into individual plugs. Dib holes between each segment of the wire mesh and put a succulent plant into each hole. Water in.
8. Leave to stand for a few weeks so that the succulents can establish before you hang the picture frame on the wall, otherwise you run the risk of the plants all falling out.

TIP... You will see the plants start to produce small babies all over their foliage, and when that happens, break them off, stick each one in a little pot of soil and they'll grow into bigger plants that can then be added to container displays.

14

MAGNETIC POT DISPLAYS

🕐 **1 HOUR**

We all have a dead space in our garden that hardly gets used, but what if you could use these traditionally useless areas for growing? Believe it or not, there is a way.

Magnetic pots are the future. We may not all have a metal space that is ripe for sticking pots to, but look a little closer and I bet you have more metallic surfaces than you think. Uprights on a balcony, railings, splash boards for barbecues, edges of water features or garden furniture? Even if you don't have these, metal panels are easy to find and fix to most surfaces. And with a huge range of magnetic pots available (or for the adventurous, strong magnets, allowing you to make your own) there is a lot of fun to be had and, crucially, a lot of practical solutions to be found with magnetic containers.

Magnetic pots do tend to be rather small, though, so don't use plants that have very deep roots or need a lot of space. Plants like strawberries work really well. Also, depending where your metallic surfaces are, your pots will either be mostly in the shade or mostly in the sun. Under the balcony, where mine are, they are in shade, so I am using an *Asplenium* (hart's tongue fern) and an *Epimedium*, both of which love shady conditions. For a sunny spot, plants like *Erigeron* or any number of herbs, including thyme, chamomile, lavender, curry plants and many more, are good. Alternatively, alpines are a great option for a sunny, exposed position. Naturally mountain dwellers, these plants can cope with extremely restricted root space, extreme brightness and extreme wind. *Raoulia, Lewisia, Lithodora* or *Veronica* are some particularly nice examples.

THE CONTAINER GARDENER

YOU WILL NEED

Plants of your choice – for edibles, strawberries and other shallow rooters will be best, for ornamentals there is a wider choice but ferns and foliage-heavy plants like ivy work really well.
Magnetic container
Multi-purpose compost
Water-retaining crystals
A metal area, either a beam or an entire wall, or get metal sheets that can be screwed to the wall

METHOD

1. Place the plants in the pot.
2. Combine the compost with the water-retaining crystals according to the packet instructions.
3. Put the compost mix around the root balls of the plants. Most of the magnetic pots you buy come without holes to avoid water dripping down the fridge and ruining your floors, so they often incorporate an internal element that raises the plant up off the base to prevent them sitting in any water.
4. Water and stick the pots to whatever metallic surface you have.
5. Water regularly, keep permanently moist but never wet.

TIP... If you really want to invest in magnetic pots and have a large metal space – maybe a corrugated iron wall of a shed or something similarly unsightly – a mass of magnetic pots can create a rather stunning living wall.

15

LIVING WALL

🕐 **A WEEKEND**

Living walls are becoming ever more popular as a solution to the problem that in our gardens a mass of green can seem out of reach because space is increasingly at a premium. They can also reduce noise pollution and can actually lower our energy bills by helping to insulate our homes from the outside.

Creating a living wall is incredibly easy; the only requirement is that you use plants that can cope with a restricted root space, and if you buy these plants as very small specimens they can be very cheap.

YOU WILL NEED

A plant hanger, made out of water-permeable liner or any other material. You can get these pre-made as fabricpouches or more robust systems made for compost bags to slide into metal hangers. Liner pouches are the cheapest option.

Wood for the frame – the cheapest wood will do; it needs to be strong but won't be seen

Rawlplugs

Screws

A sheet of strong plastic the same size as your hanger and frame

Staple gun

Sheet of thick, water-retaining fabric, such as felt

Irrigation system (optional but recommended)

Compost

Water-retaining crystals

Hooks

Plants to put in the pouches – see the Pallet living wall on page 80. Any plants with a shallow root system can cope here, whether edible or ornamental

METHOD

1. Do this with plugs in spring. Measure up the area you want to turn into a living wall. If you are using an existing wall it will need to be a strong surface, preferably one that has been waterproofed with exterior PVA or damp-proof masonry paint. It should also be strong enough to carry some weight and ideally should not be north- or directly south-facing, but a happy medium, for optimal growing conditions.

A free-standing living wall can go in front of any structure as it will not put any strain on it.

2. Build a frame out of wood, the same size as the hanging material you have made or bought. This frame needs to be a square or rectangular, depending on the size of the living wall, and supported by horizontal and vertical struts to maximise its strength. Drill it together with wood screws.

3. Attach this frame to the wall using rawlplugs and screws. This has to be really well attached as it will hold up the whole structure, which will be quite heavy once finished.

4. Fix the plastic sheet to the frame using a staple gun. You don't want any damp getting into your wall as it could cause damage to your property. Attach the water-retaining fabric over the plastic.

5. Install any irrigation systems (see Tip).

6. Attach the liner with pouches or a metal hanger to this whole structure, using screws or very strong staples.

7. Place the plants into the pouches making sure you have an even spread of textures and colours. If it is well balanced, it will grow up nicely. Alternatively, you might want to separate the colours into distinct groups with brighter plants in one area and softer plants in another.

8. Mix the compost with water-retaining crystals according to the instructions on the packet and add the compost to any gaps in the pouches. Water well.

9. Feed throughout the growing season with liquid fertiliser and water regularly.

TIP... Unless you are very diligent about watering, or your green wall is in a rainy spot, it's worth investing in an **irrigation system**. They can be bought easily and at relatively little cost. You can also get solar-powered options or attach them to water butts, to reduce your water bills.

16

CONTAINERS FOR A ROOF TERRACE

🕐 **AN AFTERNOON**

Every element that plants endure on the ground is experienced tenfold by those that are positioned above ground – on balconies or terraces, in hanging baskets or on roof gardens – because wind is stronger the higher up you go, UV rays are more intense and life is generally tougher. In high UV and high winds plants dry out very fast, so when planning a roof terrace it is important to pick species that can cope with such intense conditions (see opposite). If in doubt: 'think mountainside'. If you choose something that you recognise from a mountain, or think would look at home on a mountain – from the smallest alpine species to the largest conifer, you're heading in the right direction.

There is one other, obvious, thing to consider, and that is your pots. In high winds containers have an annoying habit of falling over, so it is often best to make or buy really sturdy pots, or, even better, to build the pots into the garden itself by integrating raised beds or, at the very least, screwing down any wooden pots. In such cases, be careful that you do not overload your roof with very heavy pots. To avoid this, fill the bottom half of the pots with polystyrene to minimise the weight and don't put more pots on the roof than can be supported. If in doubt, go for lighter pots and accept that you will need to pick them up in high winds, or even screw them down!

YOU WILL NEED

Water-retaining crystals
Compost
Plants (see opposite)
Stakes and string or rubber ties (optional)

METHOD

1. Add water-retaining crystals to your compost according to the instructions on the packet.
2. Plant your plants in raised beds or pots.
3. Stake the stems of the plants to no higher than a third of the height of the plant if it looks vulnerable to the wind. Stick a stake in the compost, preferably at a 45-degree angle, facing into the prevailing wind. Tie the plant to the stake using string or a rubber tie.
4. Water regularly at the roots rather rather than the foliage as the sun will bake any sitting water and cause the leaves to scorch.
5. It may be worth installing an irrigation system in exposed locations, as the winds can dry out your plants. This is especially useful if you have a lot of pots. Otherwise a water butt or an old barrel and watering can will do the job.
6. Regularly sweep and remove snapped stems with clean secateurs. Keep plants well watered and feed them with a mulch of composted manure, leaf mould or compost in the winter. Feed with a granular feed such as bonemeal during the summer.

PERFECT PLANTS FOR ALTITUDE

If the label on the plant isn't clear as to whether or not it will survive tougher, more exposed conditions, have a look for a few of these tell-tale signs which will point you to just the right plant.

Adaptations for high UV
Silver foliage
Chalky substance on leaves
White hairs on leaves
Low-lying foliage
Rosette formation of leaves
Bright flowers (bonus)
Little leaves
Big flowers

Adaptations for high wind
Bendy stems
Tough leaves or needles
Small foliage
Quick to regenerate after
    losing limbs!
Thick, robust trunk

17

HOMEMADE NEWSPAPER POTS

🕐 **1 HOUR**

Paper pots offer an alternative to the compostable pots available from garden centres for growing plants from seed. An essential part of seed growing is the pricking-out stage once seedlings are big enough to go into a more nutrient-rich compost and a bigger pot. Making your own paper pots is a good green option; you can use old newspapers and then recycle them once they're too soggy to use, or compost them. If you want something a little more decorative, use wrapping paper, and if you want to keep plants indoors, plants like cacti can be grown in paper bags, as they need hardly any water.

YOU WILL NEED

Paper of your choice

A tube from a toilet or kitchen roll or poster, biscuit or crisp tube – even a paper cup will do

Grit

Compost - low nutrient for seeds and cuttings

Seedlings, seeds, cuttings or plants of your choice. It is also a great way of growing seedlings and cuttings for other container projects like a hanging basket, living wall or bedding display

METHOD

1. Roll the paper around the tube or cup to cover – two layers of thickness will do but for a plant that will be there a bit longer, like a cutting, you will need more layers.
2. Fold the paper underneath at just one end.
3. Firm it down so that it stays in place and dip the bottom of the tube in water so that it holds its shape.
4. Combine the grit and compost (the ratio of the mix will depend on what plants you are growing), then fill the tubes with the mix.
5. Sow seeds into each tube, prick out seedlings into them or put in one cutting per pot. Water well.
6. When the pot becomes too soggy, either peel away the paper and pot on the pants, or plant the paper pot straight into the ground with the plant still in. It will break down and eventually supply some compost to the soil.

These are best used as greenhouse or windowsill pots, as excessive rain makes them very soggy very quickly. In a greenhouse, the pots last long enough to grow on seedlings and harden them off, then you could even plant the seedlings, in their pots, straight into the ground.

To take cuttings:

- Select healthy, non-flowering shoots from the plant.
- Cut these shoots off just above a node (leaf join).
- Trim the cut sprig to just under a leaf join.
- Remove all lower foliage just leaving the tops.
- Dib a hole in the soil and stick in the cutting.
- Water.

18

A CONCRETE JUNGLE

🕐 **A WEEKEND**

Concrete is immensely versatile. Although wet concrete or cement is toxic to plants, when fully hardened it poses no problem. And you can make your own concrete container in any shape or size.

I have put a *Phormium* in my concrete container as the beautiful, sword-like leaves give a sleek edge to this industrial pot. This container is great for any plant that has earned a thuggish reputation as many exotic, slightly 'invasives' have – running bamboo can be beautiful, but it does tend to take over and if left unchecked, *Phormium* will become enormous! One thing that stops this is concrete. So what better marriage than your homemade concrete container and your prized *Phormium* or bamboo, brought together in a way that both complements and contains them?

YOU WILL NEED

A dust sheet
A dustbin – something you don't
    mind getting mucky
An old, thick blanket
A very runny concrete mix of 3:1
    sand and cement
A bucket to mix cement in
Masonry paint and paintbrush (optional)
Exotic looking plant of your choice
Pebbles to dress the container (see tip)

METHOD

1. Lay the dust sheet on the floor with the upturned dustbin on top of it. Do this in an area of the garden that you don't mind getting messy, and do not wear your best clothes! It is also worth doing this somewhere that is protected from the worst of the rain, or pick a dry period where the forecast is rain free for at least 24 hours.
2. Dip your blanket in your runny concrete mix until it is thickly covered, then drape it over the upturned bin. Leave to dry for a minimum of 24 hours but preferably a few days.
3. Once the blanket is fully hardened, remove it from the dustbin and turn it over – it should now resemble a plant pot. At this stage you can paint the pot, if you like, using masonry paint. Move the pot to its final position now, as it will be very heavy when filled with compost and a plant. Bamboos and *Phormiums* are not fussy and can grow in nearly any position you like, preferably with a little shade during

Phormium tenax comes in a gorgeous range of different colours.

the day and the chance to catch rain drops, as they like to be moist.

4. Place your plant, still in its plastic pot, into the concrete container. There are no drainage holes in the concrete container, so you can't plant straight into it otherwise the roots will rot, and making a hole in the base could potentially let bamboo runners (if that's what you're planting) escape into the garden, which is precisely what you are trying to prevent!

5. Cover the soil surface in the plastic pot in pebbles to dress to finish the feature.

6. Water fairly regularly so that the pot never fully dries out.

TIP... Think about the colour of pebble that you use. If you have painted your container, choose a pebble that offsets that choice nicely; if not, use a grey or pale-coloured stone to harmonise with your concrete container.

19

A POND IN A METAL TROUGH

 AN AFTERNOON

We all love a pond – including the small creatures and birds that visit your garden. However, there are a couple of things that can put people off having a pond. They can be thought of as quite traditional and (dare I say) a bit messy, as well as a lot of work to build, requiring considerable outdoor space. But it is possible to have a small container pond (pot-sized!) in any corner of the garden. And if you get your container right, it can be anything but traditional. You could make one using glass, for a contemporary look that is also perfect for helping to educate young children about different habitats and insects. Here, though, I have chosen an old animal feed trough for its rustic yet geometric charm. Industrial chic meets cottage garden.

YOU WILL NEED

A fully watertight container
Hosepipe
Oxygenating plants like hornwort, spiked water milfoil or water violet
Gravel or stones
Water-loving plants (see overleaf) – go to aspecialist aquatic plant nursery, as there will be a wide choice
Upturned pots and stones to balance pots at the right depth and allow wildlife access in and out of the pond

METHOD

1. Clean the container, preferably with plain rain water, or if not, use tap water. Do not use strong chemicals as this will potentially contaminate the water and make it a hostile environment for plants.

2. Fill the container with water from a water butt. If you are using tap water you will need leave it for a few weeks before adding any fish.

3. Add oxygenating plants – these will stay submerged near the bottom.

4. Place water lilies at the bottom of the container.

5. Dress the soil surrounding your aquatic plants in their pots with gravel or stones, to weigh them down.

6. Place upturned flower pots or rocks in the water to prop up the plants you will be putting in the water.

7. Onto these place your aquatic plants, still in their pots, weighed down with gravel.

8. Move the pots around until you are happy with their arrangement.

I am using Iris laevigata, Nymphaea pygmaea (dwarf water lily) and *Equisetum fluviatile.* (Water lilies need to be dwarf varieties or they will quickly take over.)

DRAINPIPE STRAWBERRIES

 1 HOUR

The beauty of growing strawberries in a drainpipe is that it is a mutually beneficial relationship; as well as looking fantastic and fitting almost anywhere (a wall, a table edge, along the roof of your house or a shed or summer house), the strawberries actually grow better for it and taste delicious, because hanging fruits keep slugs and snails at bay. The only thing you need to do in order to ensure the best fruit is feed and water the plants regularly in early summer.

YOU WILL NEED

Some old (or new) half-pike drainpipes of the required length to fit your space
Drill and screws
Drainpipe clips to put them up
Rawlplugs, if they're going into a brick wall
Compost
Water-retaining crystals
Strawberry plants to fill the drainpipe – as a rough guide, you'll need a plant approx. every 15cm

METHOD

1. Drill holes in the drainpipes at regular 10cm intervals and attach the drainpipes to the wall with screws. If you have clips to put them up properly, attach these to the wall and hang the drainpipes onto them.
2. Attach the drainpipes to the wall screwing them through the holes. It is helpful to put them out of reach of slugs and snails, and in a spot where they will get plenty of sunshine and also some rain, to save you watering.
3. Mix the compost with the water-retaining crystals according to the instructions on the packet.
4. Place the strawberry plants into the drainpipes, 15cm apart. Fill any gaps around the plants with compost mix and water the plants well.
5. Water regularly. If it has been wet the weather should do the work for you, but remember that shallow roots dry out quickly, so water every day when it's particularly hot and dry.
6. Feed with a high-potash feed like liquid tomato feed, liquid seaweed fertiliser or comfrey tea in early summer to get the best fruit.

GRASS HEDGE IN A SCAFFOLD BOARD TROUGH

 AN AFTERNOON

Scaffold boards are lovely quality and really tough, so any projects you create with them will last a long time. As they are long, slender planks, they lend themselves to being turned into a trough – just simply screw the planks together.

Grasses are a fantastic option for these troughs. They are known as transparent plants, because you can see light through them and yet they offer privacy and seclusion. There is a wide range available, in different heights and shapes; some are erect and round while others hang and drape in elegant curves; some are eight-feet-tall, others less than one. They also come in different colours – from purples to white, silver-blues and deepest greens, offering all kinds of variegation.

YOU WILL NEED

Gloves and goggles, to protect your eyes
Claw hammer (optional)
3 scaffold boards. They come in
    lengths of 6, 8, 10 or 12ft and should
    be a standard width and depth.
    Sandpaper
Drill with 2cm wooden drill bit
Screws
Staple gun
Water-permeable liner
Multi-purpose compost with some
    sand or grit mixed in
Grasses of your choice – I used
Pennisetum macrourum, but *Miscanthus
sinesnsis, Panicum virgatum* 'Heavy Metal',
Calamagrostis acutiflora 'Karl Foerster' or
Stipa tenuissima would all work well.

METHOD

1. Remove the metal from the end of each board with a claw hammer, unless you like them as a feature, in which case, leave them on.
2. Cut a length of 178mm off two of the boards. These cut pieces will form the end pieces for your trough.
3. Cut your scaffold boards to the required length (the space you have for the trough to fit in). If you cut them carefully, you may have long enough boards to make two troughs and form a corner. If you want them as long as possible, remove 178mm from the end of the third board to give the maximum length per trough.
4. Sand the ends with sandpaper to remove any splinters and to guarantee a good finish.
5. Drill 2cm diameter holes into one of the three boards at a distance of 20cm apart. This will provide drainage.
6. Place the board with the holes in it on the ground, as this is the base of your trough.
7. In front of that board, lay another length, standing on its side, at 90 degrees from the base board, to form the front. Make sure the board is on the ground, not on the base board, to give a neater finish.
8. Screw the boards onto the base board along the front edge. You may need to brace this so that the screws go easily into the wood. Repeat with the back board.
9. You should now have a U-shaped profile. Slot your two end pieces of wood into their final positions, which will turn your U-shape into a square.

TIP... For something really special, consider growing an annual, edible grass trough in the form of barley, wheat, rice, oats or, for the most impact, a statuesque sweetcorn hedge – this will put on eight feet of growth in a year and produce delicious cobs. Better for the wildlife and better for you!

10. Screw the pieces from the front plank and the back plank with approximately four screws per side. Make sure the screws are in a neat line for a good finish.
11. Staple the liner to the inside of the container.
12. Put a 3–4cm layer of the compost mix along the bottom of the trough.
13. Place your grasses in the trough and move them around until you are happy with the effect. As grasses can be quite ephemeral, especially when they are young, arrange them fairly close together and stagger them slightly to create a thicker look. You can always thin these out after a few years if the plants get a bit crowded.
14. Using the remaining compost, fill any gaps around the roots of the plants, then water.
15. Keep moist but not wet. You shouldn't need to water too regularly as the rain will do this for you, but there will be a lot of roots which will use up water quickly. If it doesn't rain for a few days, it's worth checking the soil by feeling it. If it is dry to the touch, give the plants a quick water.
16. Feed throughout the growing season with slow-release or granular fertiliser, but don't overdo it; grasses will cope with little feeding. If you are growing sweetcorn (see tip), you will need to feed it more regularly, especially if you want healthy cobs.

22

BRICK RAISED BED FOR FERNS

A WEEKEND

Regardless of how much space you have, somewhere in among it you should include a few ferns. They tend to prefer high moisture levels and err on the shady side, though there are specialist species that prefer dry, sunny spots. Some are evergreen, while others die back in winter and flourish again in the spring, when they unfurl beautiful fronds. They all spore during the first stage of reproduction, which means they have the added interest of spore-producing fronds in the latter part of the season. The famous tree fern (*Dicksonia antarctica*) is stately and jungle-like, whereas one of my personal favourites, the hearts-tongue fern (*Asplenium scolopendrium*) is fairy-like and mysterious.

You can use pots of any kind to house your ferns, but bricks are a favourite building material for good reason, as they are relatively cheap and easy to use. If you are rendering them, you can make this project even cheaper by using concrete blocks rather than fired bricks. Once the mortar has hardened, a brick wall of any kind is an incredibly strong structure, which is important because soil or compost is heavy, especially when wet. Ferns combine beautifully with brick beds because, despite their prehistoric origins, they have a minimalist, modern look and their fronds and delicately cut leaves provide a gentleness and softness that seems to transcend fashion and trends.

YOU WILL NEED

Trowel or spade
Pointing cement trowel
Hardcore or type 1 (coarse builder's rubble)
Wacker plant (optional)
Cement
Sand
Plasticiser (washing-up liquid will do)
Bricks – either classic red or yellow bricks, breeze blocks or concrete blocks. Concrete is the cheaper option as you will need fewer of these than the smaller bricks, but because they are thinner you need more compost and soil to fill your beds. If you are not rendering the beds, bricks look vastly superior.
Spirit level
Rubber mallet
Render mix
Plastering paddle
Masonry paint and paintbrush
Compost
Topsoil
Gravel (optional)
Ferns (see opposite)

METHOD

1. Find or create an area of level ground in your garden, then dig a trench about 10cm deep and the same width as your wall will be.

2. Fill the trench with hardcore and compact it thoroughly. You might want to hire a wacker plate for this, as this layer needs to be really firm because it forms the foundation for your wall. If you have concrete on the ground, or extremely compacted soil, you may be able to skip this. If you are unsure, seek professional advice.

3. Using a mortar mix of 3:1 sand to cement, mix up a mortar. Add water until it is the consistency of ice cream – it needs to be soft enough to move and mould, but solid enough not to lose its shape. Add plasticiser (just a little squeeze per bucket load of cement) and mix in thoroughly.

4. Add mortar to the bricks as you lay them in a neat pattern, ensuring that they all stick together nicely. When laying bricks on the course below, always lay mortar on the existing wall and the brick end that points forwards so that the next brick fits snugly into an L-shaped bed of mortar and sticks well.

5. After each brick has been laid, place the spirit level on top of it and the adjoining brick, banging the top of the level with a rubber mallet until the new brick sits level.

6. Leave the mortar to dry for at least 24 hours or a few days of fine weather to ensure full dryness, if possible, then render the outer layer.

7. Using your render mix according to the packet instructions, then smooth on the render from the bottom upwards with your paddle. Push it well into the gaps and scrape it to a smooth finish. You can leave a little texture if you wish, but if not, regularly wash your paddle between applications and run it over the wall until you are happy with the result. If you are unsure about building and rendering a wall, call in a professional.

8. Paint the rendered wall once the render has dried, which will vary according to the product you use – the packet will always give clear instructions as to drying time. If you are just using a standard mortar mix you will need to wait for 2–3 fine, dry days for your render to dry, but really as long as possible. Some renders come in pre-coloured mixes, so you won't need to paint them.

9. Fill the raised bed with a mixture of compost and topsoil at a ratio of 50:50, concentrating more compost in the top 30cm of the bed. Ferns grow naturally under trees so a homemade leafmould is a cheap and brilliant growing medium for them. If you have built your raised bed on a concrete base, I would strongly recommend adding a healthy layer of gravel to the bottom of the bed (about 10cm thick) and mix gravel or sand into the compost mix in the rest of the bed.

10. Firm down the soil by stepping on the whole area (this turns the pores in the soil from macro-pores to meso-pores, helping it maintain optimum moisture levels).

11. Using a trowel or spade, plant the ferns you have chosen and water them in.

12. Keep them moist throughout the season.

↑

Remove dead or dying fronds when they appear with sharp, clean secateurs and mulch the plants with a layer of compost during the winter months to provide a rich growing medium for your ferns.

Ferns – various species for a rich assortment, including:
Dicksonia antarctica
Dryopteris spp.
Asplenium spp.
Adiantum spp.
Blechnum, for the harshest climates.
Todea barbara is a favourite of mine but will need protection from frost.

23

OUTDOOR TERRARIUM

 1 HOUR

Terrariums are fantastic little curios for the home and garden; they make a wonderful, low-maintenance container and are best suited either to small fern species, if you keep them moist, or succulent species, if you keep them dry.

Most glass containers are suitable for this project but remember that the larger your container, the more plants you need to fill it. Generally terrariums are round, as this is a really effective shape for recycling water – the glass at the top catches the condensation and allows it to drip back onto the plants. However, any shaped terrarium will do the same as long as there is enough room between the plants and the top of the glass. There is one thing that is non-negotiable – your terrarium must have a hole in it for ventilation. Whether you are growing succulents, ferns or mosses, this hole is vital to stop the container overheating and becoming too moist. In hot, moist conditions bacteria will thrive, succulents will rot and ferns will simply overheat.

YOU WILL NEED

Gravel
Funnel
Glass container with a
    ventilation hole
Multi-purpose compost
Activating charcoal
Stones
A dibber or stick
Plants of your choice
    (fern species, mosses or
    succulents work nicely)

METHOD

1. Put a layer of gravel in the bottom of the container using a funnel so that you keep the terrarium sides clean. Add compost (free from topsoil) above the gravel layer, again using a funnel. Add activating charcoal to the compost to keep the water pure.

2. Dampen the compost and gravel but don't get everything too wet, because terrariums reuse the water but do not lose an awful lot.

3. Create changes in layers to add interest to your terrarium. To do this, simply mound up the compost towards the back, adding stones to support it, to create a miniature mountainside.

4. Plant your plants with a dibber or stick as you may struggle to get your hand into the terrarium depending on the size of the container you are using.

5. Plant starting from the back and coming forward so that you don't obscure any plant when you place more in front of them.

6. Once your terrarium is planted, the plants retain water, so keep them out of the rain if possible so that you can control water levels. Shady spots are naturally dry and so are best suited for this kind of terrarium, such as at the base of a wall with rain falling from only a certain direction, or under a tree where very little rain will reach the ground. You will need to water once a week, and if you have planted succulents, you will need to water much, much less, keep it in the sun, if at all, and bring it indoors or into a greenhouse during very wet periods.

TIP... Terrariums create a micro-climate inside their glass domes, which makes it possible to grow more tender species in a temperate climate and to retain moisture in weather that would otherwise be dry. If you do grow something tender outside, though, remember that glass is not the best insulator, so you might want to protect it with a blanket or bring it indoors in winter.

My favourites include:

Succulents *Sempervivum*, *Echiveria*, *Crassula* and *Sedum*

Ferns *Dryopteris*, *Asplenium* and *Adiantum*

Moss *Selaginella*, *Lycopodium* and *Leucobryum*

24

FRUIT TREES IN CONTAINERS

🕐 **1 HOUR**

Fruit trees are not only easy to grow, but make some of the most attractive trees, particularly those in the rose family (*Rosaceae*), such as apples, cherries, pears, almonds, apricots and peaches. They produce rose-like blossom in the spring, usually ranging from white through soft pinks and into deep cerise. Many also have brightly coloured spring foliage to boot. And, of course, they all produce fruit – though not all are edible, so make sure you don't get caught out!

Lots of fruit trees in the family *Rosaceae* also produce some pretty impressive autumn colour. They are wonderful plants to grow and will flourish in a pot. In fact, a pot will restrict the growth of the tree, which means you can even grow a fruit tree on a balcony or small roof terrace.

Growing a more specialist fruit brings you a little more pride; a peach is a more unusual choice or another option (although not in the rose family) is blueberry. This is increasingly popular because blueberries are so good for you, the plants are also fully hardy and easy to grow, and because they need an ericaceous – or acidic – soil. If you don't have this type of soil you will have to grow them in a pot anyway.

YOU WILL NEED

Multi-purpose compost (Ericaceous for a blueberry)
Slow-release fertiliser – a manure such as pelleted chicken manure or seasoned horse or cow manure, or a granular form of fertiliser
Crocks
A pot – any kind will do, but generally get the largest pot you can accommodate/afford as more soil means it will offer more valuable nutrients for flowers and fruit
A peach tree – research a variety that you know to be very tasty. 'Arctic Supreme', 'Belle of Georgia' and 'Empress' (a dwarf specimen) are some of the best.
Gravel for dressing the pot

METHOD

1. Mix the compost with the fertiliser, according to the packet instructions.
2. Place a layer of crocks into the pot and add a layer of compost mix.
3. Position the peach tree in the pot and backfill with the remaining compost. Firm the soil by pushing down on the surface of the compost around the roots of the plant with your hands, then water in well.
4. Feed throughout the growing season, especially when fruit is developing, with a potash-rich liquid fertiliser and add granular or other slow-release fertiliser during the winter.
5. If you get lots and lots of fruit you must thin them a little as the year progresses. In most cases, but especially when nutrients are restricted, as they are in a pot, a plant does not have the energy to ripen hundreds of delicious, big and juicy fruit, so instead it will make loads of small, less tasty ones; reducing the number of fruits means the ones that do develop will be bigger, tastier and juicier.
6. You may need to bring the pot indoors or into a greenhouse or sheltered space during any frosts. Some fruit trees are hardy but check your cultivar for specific information.

Pollinating your fruit tree
If you only have one plant, you
may want to ensure pollination
by going from flower to flower
with a paintbrush. You need
to do this in the spring when
the plant is in blossom. Using
the tip of a clean paintbrush,
brush the pollen on the end
of the stamens and then go
to a different flower on the
same plant and brush that
pollen onto the stigma. The
more flowers you manage to
fertilise, the more fruit you
will get later in the year.

25

A TROPICAL STACK FOR A DULL CORNER

🕐 AN AFTERNOON

This display is fully hardy and can make any space feel tropical. It works best on a patio, particularly near your al fresco dining table – I always think that eating in a space that feels tropical creates the illusion of warm summer evenings. You don't need somewhere warm to grow a display that looks tropical, but if it is and is free from frost and yet moist enough to support plant life, you could substitute these plant choices with some more tender alternatives, such as *Dahlias*, *Cannas*, bananas and real gingers rather than the hardy ornamental version. However, for the purposes of general usefulness, as not all of us are lucky enough to live in warm climes, I have used species that are tolerant of a temperate climate.

You can use nearly any kind of container to create this feature, but because this project also cleverly incorporates height into your garden, one container must be significantly bigger than the other two (about twice the size) to allow a good planting space around the base of the small container. Only your large container will be seen, so choose a nice one. If you are looking to save a bit of money, you can use any old container for the smaller central pot and hide a strong plastic one right inside the big pot.

YOU WILL NEED

Three big containers,
  two smaller ones about half
  the size of one big one
Another container to balance
  the smaller one on
Crocks
Compost
Water-retaining crystals
Granular feed
Plants (see below)

METHOD

1. It is best to build this container display in its final position as it is a heavy structure and is potentially a little unstable until the roots of the plants have grown to support it.
2. Place an upturned container in the base of the big container.
3. On top of that place the other smaller container – it doesn't have to be beautiful as this one will be hidden by planting.
4. Place a layer of crocks in both upright containers.
5. Mix the compost with the water-retaining crystals and granular feed as directed on the packet instructions.
6. Nearly fill the larger container with compost and add a little to the smaller container.
7. Plant your tallest plant in the smaller container and backfill with more compost.
8. Plant the large container so that it is really filled, colourful and lush. Once you are happy, backfill any gaps with the remaining compost. Water well.
9. Feed throughout the growing season with a granular feed.
10. Cut back the herbaceous plants in the autumn.
11. Prune the shrubs for shape and to remove any dead or diseased material as needed.

← I've chosen *Fatsia japonica* for this and smaller plants for the lower level. I've chosen a heavily toothed elder, *Hedychium* (ornamental ginger), *Rudbeckia*, *Geranium*, *Hebe*.

A POTTED BONSAI FOREST

Bonsai, or *penjing*, as it is known in China, is the ancient oriental practice of restricting a tree's growth by keeping it in a pot. Specimens can live for centuries as perfect miniature replicas of their larger brothers. If you are a nurturing, careful person, this is for you. If you are more a type who likes to throw things in a pot or in the ground and let nature take care of the rest, it's best to steer clear of the ancient art of bonsai.

If you are growing bonsai trees, I would highly recommend getting containers specifically designed for this purpose. Trees have roots that grow in a very precise way and a bonsai container is wide and shallow to mimic this shape – think of a wine glass with the tree canopy taking up the goblet and the roots taking up the space of the base. A very deep pot will contain a lot of wasted compost. Bonsai pots also tend to be glazed so that they retain more water.

YOU WILL NEED

A bonsai tree in a pot
Bonsai pruning clippers

METHOD

1. Water only when the soil has begun to get dry and make sure it has soaked right the way through the soil. Either soak the plant and pot in a bucket or in the sink, or water from above until water runs through the base of the pot, then repeat a few minutes later.
2. Feeding is also an important part of bonsai maintenance. You should fertilise through the growing season (spring to autumn) and buy products specifically for bonsai trees.
3. Pruning is also essential. Mainly, in bonsai care, the pruning is of the roots rather than the tips of the trees. However, always remove any dead or diseased branches and any branches that cross or rub together, and you may want to remove a branch that is unsightly occasionally.
4. For bonsai, the soil type you use is crucial, so make sure you buy compost specifically for bonsai. There is also an element of pushing a bonsai tree to its limits, so do not re-pot too frequently – every few years will do – or your tree will begin to get bigger and less and less like a bonsai.

CUT FLOWERS IN AN UPCYCLED CRATE

🕐 AN AFTERNOON

Any flowers can be cut to decorate our homes but there are certain species that are especially suitable, such as flowers with strong, long stems which stay healthy for longer in our vases. Then there are more subjective qualities, such as colours that you admire or even scents that you prefer. Having a dedicated area in which to grow flowers in succession means you can cut blooms throughout the seasons. You can do this by growing different flowers in the same container that will bloom at different times, but you will have to plan your pots to achieve this. You also need to choose species so they complement each other when they come into flower; there is no point having a sunflower and a soft yellow lily, for example, that bloom at the same time but look awful next to each other. There is a degree of skill in planning a successful container for cut flowers, but one way of getting around the problems of succession and beautifully matched plants is having more than one container. One for each room of your house, perhaps, or one for hot combinations and one for cool. This way you can have the best of both worlds.

In terms of flower choice, think texture. Different textures complement each other, so a fern frond, or a sprig of eucalyptus or even a gently frothing *Gypsophila* might be just the thing to really make your rose blooms stand out. Think about all these different elements to create a really successful scheme, but, crucially, to create a grouping of plants that you love!

TIP... You might find it best, unlike in any other planting schemes, to grow these flowers as you would your vegetables – in rows. If you have them planted in big groups or rows, you always know that you're getting the right flower type, even if the buds haven't quite opened yet, and you have the joy of arranging them beautifully, rather than trying to mimic the natural look of what you already had growing.

YOU WILL NEED

A large wooden crate. It needs to be
    big enough to accommodate a
    few different flower species, and
    deep enough to grow bulbs and
    herbaceous perennials.
Plastic liner
Staple gun
Scissors
Compost
Plants
Bulbs
Granular or any slow-release fertiliser

Combine plants to create
a diverse succession of
complementary species.
Choose colours and species
that you like best as they will
end up in your home and not
just your garden.

Bulbs
Tulipa 'Queen of the Night'
Narcissus 'Silver Chimes'
Allium caeruleum
Annual seeds
Poppy
Nigella
Cornflower
Perennials
Pink roses
Helenium
Dianthus

METHOD

1. It is best to begin this project in autumn, to maximise production for the following year. Plant up the crate in its final position and, if possible, choose a location that is mostly protected from the wind. You want the flower stems to be able to grow tall and straight, without any damage, so choose a sheltered position if you can. Also make sure there is some sun throughout the day so that the stems can grow straight upwards rather than leaning out to find light.

2. Line your container with the plastic liner, using the staple gun to attach it to the sides.

3. Cut holes in the liner at the base to allow drainage.

4. Fill your container with compost up to 15cm from the surface.

5. Lay out rows of the bulbs. In between

these rows, lay rows of herbaceous plants. Backfill with the remaining compost.

6. Feed in the spring with manure pellets or another slow-release fertiliser, following the instructions on the packet.

7. Chop back any late-flowering perennials in mid-spring (reduce the growth by half). If you would like more blooms, remember they will be smaller than those not cut back, so you may want to only cut half of them back for a good succession of cut flowers.

8. In spring, sow summer annuals for later in the year (apart from sweet peas, which can often be more successful if sown the autumn before).

9. Remove flower stems from bulbs when the buds are on the verge of opening.

10. Always cut stems on the diagonal and put them in clean water with plant food to reduce risk of bacterial infection and maximise the life of your cut flower displays.

11. Once the bulbs have all gone over, plant out annual bedding in the rows where the bulbs used to be.

12. Keep moist throughout the summer. Deadhead regularly to keep the flowers blooming.

13. When putting cut flowers in water always remove lower foliage.

BULB DISPLAY IN PAINTED POTS

🕐 **1 HOUR**

Bulbs are the container-lover's best friends. They grow in nearly any soil type and need minimal care, and if you choose your species carefully, they will come back year after year. For some of the more beautiful bulbs, such as tulips, there is a little more effort required and they may need replacing every two years, otherwise they tend to get smaller and smaller until they stop coming back altogether.

Nowadays we tend to prefer the less bright and bold bulb displays. I still think the cheer and unashamed punch in the face of colour that you get from these bulbs is delightful. But with careful choices you can create a feature that is much more tasteful, subtle and elegant, and one that will keep coming back with minimal effort. Painting your flower pots may seem extremely obvious, but in actual fact it is a hugely effective twist on the traditional.

↑

My favourite bulbs include: *Allium hollandicum* 'Purple Sensation', *Fritillaria meleagris*, *Nectaroscordum*, *Camassia* (pink or white), *Narcissus* 'Thalia', *Chionodoxa luciliae*

YOU WILL NEED

Traditional terracotta pots (any kind, not necessarily the old, rustic ones)
Paint and paintbrush – any tough-wearing paint will do. If you want really bright colours, acrylic might provide the greatest variety, but if you want classic, more subdued colours, an exterior masonry paint is the most hardwearing
Crocks
Multi-purpose compost
Bulbs

METHOD

1. It is best to begin this project in autumn when you can buy bulbs, rather than in the spring when the bulbs are already in flower and are much more expensive as well as less likely to come back the following year, looking lovely and healthy. Snowdrops are the only exception as they need to be bought ready grown in compost – 'in the green' as it is known.

2. Paint the bottom or top half to two-thirds of your pots, depending on taste and colour. If you have chosen a very bright colour (though you may then want to consider changing the bulb choices to something a little less pastel), you can paint the whole pot. Anything with an element of subtlety, such as pale pink, lilac, white, pale blue, duck egg, grey or even navy (especially with the terracotta colour) will work nicely if the pot is half painted. You could always try painting half then go on to paint the whole thing if you feel the colour combination isn't working.

3. Place a couple of pieces of crocks, or even just a few stones, in the bottom of the pot – most bulbs hate to sit in water, as it can cause them to rot, especially in winter, so it's best to add extra drainage. You may even want to include some gravel if you are worried about this or live in an area with high rainfall.

4. Add compost to the pot until it's about 15cm from the top.

5. Place the biggest bulbs on this layer –

so that's the *Alliums* and the *Camassias*. It is a good rule of thumb that any bulb should generally be planted at a depth of three times its height. There are a few exceptions, such as hyacinths, which need to be planted on the surface to encourage flowers, but generally speaking you can't go far wrong by following this rule. If in doubt, most packets will have planting depths written on the back.

6. Pour a layer of compost over the top of the bulbs until the soil is at a depth of about 10cm.

7. Arrange a layer of *Narcissus* and *Nectaroscordum*. Add yet more compost until there is about 5cm of the pot rim showing.

8. There is no need to water the pots if they are left outside because the weather should do this for you over the winter months.

9. Feed the bulbs as they are growing with a granular organic fertiliser, which should be watered in. Remove any seedheads before they have a chance to fully form. Remove the dead stems once they have turned completely brown and replenish the compost with a bit of fresh compost every year.

10. You may want to add some extra bulbs every autumn to keep your displays looking their best year on year. You should replace any tulips that have finished flowering, or add extra ones because over a few years the tulips will become weaker.

PICTURE FRAME SEEDLINGS

🕐 **AN AFTERNOON**

We gardeners take great pride in our plants, and although we secretly like to think of our gardens and our plants as works of art, it is not usually the norm to put them in a picture frame. But this method of growing seedlings is a really good way of seeing them in their full glory. By growing your seeds like this you get to see them at every stage of growth, from germination to emersion and right up to the point when they are ready to be pricked out. Anything with shallow roots, such as alpines, succulents, Mediterranean herbs and mosses, would be happy in a container like this as long as it is kept well watered. It's a really fun way of engaging kids in the process of growing while also educating them about nature and science. It's infinitely fascinating for us adults, too!

YOU WILL NEED

A piece of thin plywood
A picture frame at least 3cm deep, picture and glass removed
Some waterproof paint (any colour you like, but darker colours work particularly well)
Paintbrush
Perspex (cut to two thirds the height of the picture frame)
A drill
Screws
Hooks to hang the picture
Strong exterior wire
Picture hook
Hammer
Nail
Seed compost (or multi-purpose if you are growing something else)
Seeds of your choice

METHOD

1. Cut a piece of plywood the same size as the back of the picture frame.
2. Paint the plywood and the inside of the frame with your chosen colour and leave to dry for 2 hours or until the paint is bone dry. Any dampness will mean that soil sticks to the paint.
3. Insert the Perspex into the place where the glass would normally go, ensuring the gap is at the top.
4. Screw the plywood to the back of the frame using a drill and wood screws.
5. Drill three to four drainage holes into the underside of the frame.
6. Attach the hooks and wire to the back of the picture frame. Usually hooks and eyes for picture frames screw in on their own, so you can do this by hand rather than using a drill. Thread the wire through and double it back on itself, twisting it around itself.
7. Put a picture hook in the wall using a hammer and nail.
8. Hang up the frame, putting the middle point of the wire on the hook and making sure it is level.
9. Fill the frame with soil, leaving a gap of a few centimetres at the top.
10. Sprinkle or sow your seeds following the instructions on the seed packets. Water well and make sure they stay moist. Watch them grow!
11. Prick out the seedlings once the second set of leaves has grown. If you have left a third of the top space free, you should be able to do this with a dibber or a pencil. Otherwise, carefully remove the frame from the wall and unscrew the plywood so that you can access the seedlings.

For extra healthy edibles, grow micro greens in your picture frame and harvest them at this stage. Coriander, peashoots, radish, cabbage, leek, mustard work well like this.

AN OLD CABINET WITH BURNT ORANGE AND BLUES

 AN AFTERNOON

What could be more magical, or unusual, than furniture turned into a container? We all have old pieces in our homes or sheds that we no longer use, so it's time to resurrect them and turn them into something new. This project works best with a chest of drawers, but any cabinet can be turned into something useful and beautiful.

Wooden furniture will probably need a regular coat of varnish or preserver if you want it to have a long life in your garden, before you plant it up. I love blue and orange – they evoke a sense of rustiness and look eclectically modern; natural but strangely unnatural. These are contrasting colours and very few plants are naturally bright blue, making them feel unearthly, yet the rusty colours of the burnt orange anchor a scheme very much in nature. For an old cabinet this is a great combination of colours and makes it a really striking design feature.

YOU WILL NEED

Old chest of drawers or cabinet of any size, to fit the space you have to fill. It can be made of wood (remember this needs treating to protect it from the elements), metal or plastic. One with three drawers works best, to allow the plants plenty of room to grow.
Wood preserver and paintbrush
Drill
Plastic liner
Screws and screwdriver
Multi-purpose compost
Plants

I'm using blues and oranges:
Eryngium
Agapanthus
Lobelia erinus 'Blue Cascade'
Festuca glauca 'Elijah Blue'
Carex 'Red Rooster'
Crocosmia (common montbretia)
Ceratostigma
Anemanthele lessoniana
Hardy blue *Geranium*
Lavandula angustifolia
Libertia peregrinans

METHOD

1. Remove the drawers. If you are using a wooden cabinet, treat the whole cabinet with varnish or wood preserver.

2. Drill drainage holes into each drawer at intervals of about 7cm.

3. Line each drawer that you intend to plant up with plastic and make holes in the liner that correspond with the holes in the drawer. If you have a classic three-drawer chest, the best way to plant it up is by planting the top and bottom drawers but leaving the middle drawer unplanted, for reasons of weight distribution.

4. Replace the drawers with the lowest one sticking out the furthest and the top one only open the equivalent to the width of one plant.

5. Screw the drawers into position so there is no chance of them falling out once weighed down with plants

6. Fill each drawer with compost.

7. Arrange your plants in the drawers, making sure the cascading plants, such as hardy *Geranium*, disguise the edges. Water in.

8. Keep your plants moist throughout the season by watering them during dry, hot periods. There is little need to deadhead these species, with the exception of the *Lobelia*; if you keep the flower seeds on for as long as possible into the winter it will provide food for the birds.

For extra security weigh or screw down your cabinet to stop it falling over.

A WINTER POT

🕐 **AN AFTERNOON**

It is a strange phenomenon that the most scented plants grow best in shade. This is because in the dark shadows of trees insects struggle to see flowers, so if plants can lure insects with their sweet smells, there is more chance of them being pollinated. Often shade-lovers will also have white flowers to make them as visible as possible, and the combination of white flowers and a heady scent can make a great feature. What better way to make use of a shady corner of the garden? There are also a host of plants that flower in the winter or late autumn that give a delicate splash of colour in the depths of the season.

Here I've planted one such flowering plant, *Chrysanthemum*, in a pot made of cement, that I created using a wok as my mould and a dryish cement mix. The beauty of this is that in shady conditions it will grow a rich layer of moss on it, creating a beautifully natural and aged look.

YOU WILL NEED

A stone trough – something that will age nicely and get a lovely covering of moss in time. If you don't have a stone container you can make your own using concrete, a petroleum jelly and a wok (see method)
Multi-purpose compost
Plants

METHOD

1. Mix some mortar to make a dryish, still grainy and definitely not wet mix.
2. Cover an old wok in petroleum jelly.
3. Line the wok with mortar mix around 3–4cm thick. Leave a hole in the centre for drainage – this will be doable if your cement mix is dry enough.
4. After 48 hours of dry conditions, remove the concrete from the wok. It should fall out easily if there was enough petroleum jelly in the wok.

HOW TO PLANT

1. If you are planting a single specimen like the *Chrysanthemum* then place it in isolation in the pot. The round form of the *Chrysanthemum* will echo the rounded shape of the wok. It makes a fantastic impact.
2. Keep the compost moist but not wet and feed with a granular fertiliser every few months.
3. Place the stone trough in a corner of the garden that gets shade or partial sun. If the wall or fence above it gets more sun, then a clematis will flower prolifically. (If there is no sun, replace the clematis with ivy – the flowers may not be as strongly scented, but at the end of the summer they provide some perfume and the bees go mad for them.)
4. Fill the trough with compost nearly to the top.
5. Plant the clematis at the back and attach it to the wall behind. In front of the clematis, plant the *Daphne odora*. Fill the whole of the front of the trough with lily-of-the-valley, then water in. If you have made the container using a wok, leave out the clematis as this needs deep rooting space which this homemade stone trough won't provide.
6. As the plants in this container are fairly long lived, you need to replace the compost every few years, and pot the plants on every five or so years, to allow each species plenty of growing room. If you have not got the room to do this, just growing a *Daphne odora* or a lily-of-the-valley will provide shady scent without the need for regular potting on.

For winter scent
Daphne odora
Convallaria majalis
    (lily-of-the-valley)
Clematis armandii
For winter flower
Chrysathemum
Galanthus nivalis
Winter aconite
Primula
Cyclamen hederifolium

32

A RUSTIC STONE POT FILLED WITH ACID-LOVING PLANTS

🕐 **1 HOUR**

There are different kinds of soil and each type makes a perfect home for different kinds of plants. Acid soil is one of the most common, and most plants prefer soil to be ever so slightly acidic rather than ever so slightly alkaline. When we talk about acid-lovers, though, we mean plants that really need acidic conditions, or at least plants that are pretty uncomfortable in an alkaline soil. To get an idea of these species you need to imagine a moor, a heath or a mountain. In these conditions, where the soil is in close proximity to the rock below (unless that rock is a form of limestone), the soil will tend to be very acidic. Anything that grows there will grow in your acidic pot. We typically think of *Rhododendrons*, *Camellias* and other such species for these conditions, but there are other, more interesting species, that prefer an acidic position, too. To recreate this moor in the garden, I have devised a project that is rustic and naturalistic to create a little piece of acid heaven.

Using stones

Porous stones hold on to more moisture, but use whatever stones you have in your area, as this makes buying them cheaper and they look more at home in your garden. Alternatively, if you have paved areas, match the stones to your paving. The only stones that are not appropriate are limestones, as these are alkaline and will affect the health of the acid-loving plants.

YOU WILL NEED

Stones – quite big and flat, though any kind will do. You will need more stones if they are smaller or if you have a large space, fewer if they are big or you have a smaller space.
Ericaceous compost
Acid-loving plant: *Acer, Pieris, Erica, Dryopteris* (or any others you like, including *Magnolia, Cedrus, Ceanothus, Molinia, Loropetalum, Cornus, Viburnum, Sorbus, Skimmia* and many more)

METHOD

1. Arrange your stones in a circular shape and build up to a height that you feel is stable and secure to make a container. (You can shore it up with mortar, if you like, but this will decrease its acidity.) You will need to protect the *Acer* and the ferns from full sunshine and strong winds, so place the stone circle in a suitable position.
2. Fill the stone container, including any gaps in the stones, with ericaceous compost, nearly to the top.
3. Plant your chosen species into the container, including in the gaps in the stones, then water well.
4. Add a mulch of ericaceous compost every year to keep the species looking healthy. Prune when required to ensure the shape of your plants stays attractive and remove any dead, dying or diseased branches.

To ring the changes, you could try one of these different planting combinations:

Acer, *Pieris* and *Loropetalum chinense*.

Ceanothus, *Dryopteris* (keep it simple with blues and greens).

Cornus with *Molinia* – something with a red coloration like 'Edith Dudszus' looks breathtaking against the red stems of a *Cornus alba*.

Sorbus aucuparia ('Copper Kettle' is beautiful, S. *vilmorinii* is a personal favourite, or the classic, red berries of mountain ash look great) with *Molinia* and *Erica* in drifts looks fantastic in a large container.

Cedrus glauca gets huge in the ground but its growth is restricted in a pot, and it looks wonderful underplanted with shade-tolerant ferns such as *Dryopteris* and white-flowered *Calluna*.

33

TURN YOUR WHEELIE BIN INTO SOMETHING MORE PRODUCTIVE

🕐 **1 HOUR**

The wheelie bin has become as much a part of our household as the family pet. It often jostles with the car for the limited space in front of our homes (and your partner's car and the cars of anyone who comes to visit). We often try to come up with ingenious ways of hiding these eyesores and spend considerable amounts of money doing so. Sheds are built around them, stickers go on their sides, fences are erected in front of them. But the way I see it, these bins are essentially huge containers, so rather than going to great lengths to try to hide them, flaunt them. Not the ones you need for your rubbish and recycling, but the ones you might have left over. When your local authority redesigns the bins, for instance, or if one of your bins gets a little broken or develops a hole, so much the better. There are a number of vegetables that positively thrive in such conditions, particularly ones that grow long in either direction, such as root veg like parsnips and carrots, as well as the leafy vegetable I'm focusing on – leeks.

YOU WILL NEED

Old wheelie bin at least 1m tall
Drill
Multi-purpose compost
Dibber
Leeks (pencil thickness, ready to plant –
    either seedlings you've grown yourself
    or ones you've bought. Sow leeks in
    spring and plant them out into their
    final position in early summer.)
Granular slow-release fertiliser

METHOD

1. Drill some drainage holes into the bottom of your old wheelie bin – four decent-sized holes should be enough to let excess water escape.
2. Fill the bin with compost up to about three-fifths full or just over halfway. Firm the compost.
3. With a dibber, make holes in the soil about 15cm apart and drop one leek into each – you will probably fit about nine leeks into each wheelie bin.
4. Water and feed them regularly throughout the growing season with a high-nitrogen fertiliser such as chicken manure pellets.
5. Harvest the leeks from the end of the summer right through the winter, when they will be big enough to eat, but before they have gone to flower.

UPCYCLED CHAIR WITH DEEP PURPLES AND SILVERS

🕐 **AN AFTERNOON**

There is a lot of aesthetic value in old furniture, and even modern pieces have something to offer, if you have the vision to turn them into something more interesting. What better way to revitalise them than to mix antique pieces with something natural? Chairs make really good upcycled containers because, as well as adding greenery, you are adding a bit of sculpture and height to your garden. Creating varying levels keeps the eye interested, which can really bring a small space to life.

A purple and silver planting combination is ever-so-slightly magical. Plants in these colours tend to have a certain delicacy that others lack. Plants with silver foliage go well with any other colour and provide interest even when they are not in flower. In a small space like a container, where plant choices are limited, this adds a great deal of aesthetic value. Pale colours, such as silver, also reflect light and bounce well off other colours without stealing the show. Purple marries effortlessly and naturally with silver, and echoes this dainty style, with flowerheads from *Alliums* and little *Campanula* creating the same fairy-like feel. You could also use any bright colour.

Bulbs

Allium hollandicum 'Purple Sensation'
Tulipa 'Queen of Night'
Iris reticulata 'Katharine Hodgkin'
Heuchera 'Palace Purple'
Sedum sieboldii

Perennial plants

Artemisia schmidtiana
Verbena bonariensis
Nepeta x *faassenii*

YOU WILL NEED

An old chair – wood or metal works best as it can withstand the weather. If you have an old upholstered chair you can use that, but it will become damp and probably mouldy in time, maybe even sprouting some fungi after a season or two. If you don't mind it rotting to nothing quickly, use it, otherwise I would stick to wood or metal

Strong hessian sacking
Drill
Compost
Water-retaining crystals
Bulbs and perennial plants (see left)
Staple gun

METHOD

1. Start this project in the autumn when bulbs are at their cheapest and there is a few months for them to settle in. Remove the seat of the chair by cutting it off and lifting it out. Some wooden seats can simply be prised off. Avoid damaging the chair itself.

2. Make a strong, deep bowl of hessian sacking (strong enough to house plants, compost and water) where the seat was. You may need to double or even triple the layers of hessian in order to guarantee its strength. Staple it to the seat.

3. Mix the compost with the water-retaining crystals according to the packet instructions.

4. Put a thin layer of compost in the bottom of your container.

5. Place the *Alliums* and tulips on the layer of compost. Sprinkle more compost on the top so that the bulbs are nearly covered.

6. Around the bulbs, place your perennial plants (be careful to allow the bulbs beneath space to grow up, so try to avoid putting perennials directly on top of them).

7. Fill the spaces around the root balls with the remaining compost.

8. Into the gaps between the plants, push the *Iris reticulata,* very gently so that you don't damage them.

9. Water the plants well. Keep the soil moist but not wet – these plants like fairly dry conditions. (It is important, as ever, in containers to choose plants that complement each other in terms of their preferred conditions.)

10. In the spring and summer, as soon as the bulbs have gone brown, cut off the foliage to make the best summer display.

MOSS TEACUPS

🕐 **1 HOUR**

Moss is in high demand. Garden designers who have been using cushion moss in Japanese-inspired reflection gardens and alongside large cobbles have inspired the horticultural world. However, it is important to acquire moss from sustainable sources; it is illegal to collect it from the woods, as a means of protecting native species in the wild. You can buy sustainably grown moss from all sorts of places, it is even being introduced across prison systems as a way of encouraging free enterprise for prisoners, and there has been a lot of research into growing it sustainably, so do support these endeavours.

Teacups make a great feature on their own; I love teacups and have an unfortunate habit of collecting them. I also make pottery, especially teacups, so I find my collection is growing to unsustainable numbers! As a way of using them more effectively, I have started to grow plants in them. Moss is a great choice for this because the cups offer such a limited space and I love the lush, verdant and varying choice it provides.

YOU WILL NEED

An old china teacup and saucer
Moisture-retentive soil or compost
Sustainably sourced moss. The most attractive mosses for a container include cushion moss (*Leucobryum*), upright moss (*Polytrichum*), sphagnum moss (*Sphagnum*), club moss (*Lycopodium*) and spike moss (*Selaginella*), though there are many more interesting species if you can find a specialist grower

METHOD

1. Fill the cup with the soil or compost. Generally, moss likes the shade, where it is damp. You might find that compost-filled cups just left around shady areas of the garden naturally begin to form moss of their own, but if you have bought moss, and are in doubt about where to put your container, damp shade is usually best.
2. Place the moss carefully on top of the soil.
3. Give the whole thing a good water.
4. It will need to be kept permanently moist but not wet, so keep an eye on it.

36

UPCYCLED CONTAINER CHAIRS

 AN AFTERNOON

Garden furniture, like it or loath it, has become part of our daily lives. Housing is becoming ever more expensive and we often find ourselves struggling with limited space. Outdoor areas are therefore increasingly precious and we have begun to use them as an extension of our homes. We eat outside, sit outside, some people even sleep outside from time to time. A garden gives us extra room, but all too often the furniture we have can be something of an eyesore. There are some lovely pieces of outdoor furniture available if you are willing to spend a lot, but the cheaper they are the less stylish they tend to be, however useful. So here's a good solution: why not try making your own, home-grown outdoor furniture? There are all sorts of plants you can sit or lie on. Some, like chamomile, are beautifully scented and can be used in all sorts of ways, from cosmetics to tea, and can be grown on all sorts of surfaces, to make all kinds of ingenious seating. So with practicality and beauty to gain, there isn't much to lose. I'm using thyme, which is incidentally one of my favourite culinary herbs too!

YOU WILL NEED

Piece of old plywood
Pen/pencil
Saw
An old car tyre – you can pick these up easily from garages or scrapyards at very little cost
Screws
Drill
Gravel
Compost
Chamomile, or another plant that can be trampled, such as thyme or even turf

METHOD

1. Cut the plywood into a circle to fit the tyre – measure it by placing the tyre on top of the wood and drawing around it - a hexagon works as well as a circle and is easier to cut! For an extra long life, you might want to varnish your plywood.

2. Screw the plywood onto the tyre, using wood screws that go through the plywood and straight into the tyre.

3. Drill some holes into the plywood for drainage every 7cm or so – most trample-proof plants require a free-draining compost so you can't overdo the holes as long as you don't compromise the strength of the plywood.

4. Mix the compost with the gravel in a 50:50 mix.

5. Pour the compost into the tyre so that it is nearly at the top. Firm it down well.

6. Make small holes in the compost and put the plants into the holes so that there is good coverage but still a few centimetres around each plant for the roots to grow. Water in.

7. Keep watered but not too much – if the seat is outside, the rain should do the job.

FIVE WAYS TO TRANSFORM A PLASTIC POT

We all have plastic pots lying around and, annoyingly, every time we buy another plant we get another pot. But with a little ingenuity and creativity you can turn them into something much more beautiful. It doesn't take a lot of time or skill, just a few simple tricks will make your plastic pots into something to be proud of.

Generally, giving these pots a face lift requires some messy materials, so you may want to lay down newspaper or plastic sheets before you begin. The most basic method of transformation is painting; it's simple and effective, and by layering and distressing the paint you can create a brilliant and quite expensive-looking container. For a more specialist look, painted pots can be adorned with words – perhaps your name, or a quote or phrase that means a lot to you. More skilful painters can do this by hand but a stencil will work just as well.

The next step up from painting is sticking things to your pots. It may sound a bit pre-school, but it can actually look very attractive. With a paper napkin, a bit of old string, or some sand, the transformation becomes easy and effective.

DÉCOUPAGE WITH NAPKINS ⏱ A WEEKEND

WHAT YOU WILL NEED

Paper napkins – plain or patterned,
    depending on your taste
Plastic pots
Waterproof PVA glue
    (suitable for exteriors)
Paintbrush

METHOD

1. Tear or cut the paper napkins into thin strips. The smaller the strips the neater it will be, but using big pieces creates more texture and gets the job done quicker.

2. Cover the pot in waterproof PVA with a paintbrush. Stick a layer of napkin strips all over the pot. Cover the layer of napkins with PVA glue using a paintbrush. Stick on another layer of torn-up napkins, then coat with another layer of PVA glue.

3. Leave to dry – this should take 12–24 hours, depending on the conditions.

4. Plant it up with any plants you like. For heavily decorative découpage, foliage-driven planting like alpines, (I've used *Raoulia*) or even mosses work really nicely, but for more simple designs, you can let the plants and flowers speak for themselves by using shrubs with interesting foliage colour and plants with flowers. Scents are great, either foliage or flower, no matter what colour and pattern your paper is.

Clockwise from top left: Moss, *Raoulia*, *Cotinus* in découpage pots.

PROJECTS

147

PAINTED AND AGED ⏱ AN AFTERNOON

YOU WILL NEED

Plastic pots
Paintbrush
Paint (waterproof or exterior –
    masonry works best.
    Two related but slight
    different tones will create
    an aged look)
Old fork or steel wool
Sponge

METHOD

1. Paint on a thick layer of colour – greys and whites work best as closely related colours blend well. Grey creates a stone-like effect, while bright colours are more unnatural, but more fun and unusual.

2. Using an old fork or some steel wool, remove and cross-hatch parts of the paint while it's still wet.

3. Once the paint has dried (it should take a couple of hours but check the paint tub for timings), stipple on extra colour with the sponge. A slightly different tone works really nicely to create a naturally aged finish. Once this layer has dried, you may want to go over patches with the original colour to even out the tone.

4. Plant up with any plant of your choice. When it comes to plastic pots, the simpler the plant the better, especially if your pot has been adorned. Whether you have gone for a natural stone finish or a brighter, more exotic look – something like a fern or other foliage plant, such as *Pachysandra terminalis* or *Vinca minor* with its sporadic, blue flowers, will enhance the pot without making the whole arrangement too fussy.

STENCILLED LETTERS ⏱ AN AFTERNOON

YOU WILL NEED

Plastic pots
Multi-purpose spray paint
(available from most
hardware stores in all
kinds of colours)
Stencils
Sponge (optional)
Waterproof paint (optional)

METHOD

1. Spray the pot with multi-purpose spray paint. To avoid this becoming too cheesy you might want to pick tasteful, subtle colours; white on a pale blue background works nicely, or grey on white. If you are making named pots, particularly for children, get them to choose their colours to make it even more personal.

2. Choose a word or phrase you want to feature; it could be the name of the plant you intend to grow – herb collections work really well like that, for example – or the name of the person who will be using the pot, it could be your house name or number if you intend to put the pot by the front door.

3. Stencil the chosen word to the front of the pot using spray paint in a contrasting colour or a sponge dipped in waterproof paint.

4. Wait 2–4 hours for the container to dry. (Always check the paint tub for specific drying times.)

5. Plant up with the plants of your choice. As the pot is decorative, keeping the planting simple creates a really effective feature. Your colour schemes will also dictate your planting; green goes with any bright colour, so foliage-led design will enhance the pot, whereas contrasting colours create a really zingy look. A purple pot is brought to life with yellow flowers, orange goes with blue, and so on.

SANDBLASTED 🕐 A WEEKEND

YOU WILL NEED

Plastic pots
Waterproof PVA glue
   (suitable for exteriors)
Paintbrush
Sand
Ribbon or string (optional)

METHOD

1. Cover your plastic pot in waterproof PVA glue using a paintbrush.
2. Roll the glue-covered pot in your chosen sand.
3. Wait up to 24 hours for it to dry and set.
4. Plant it up. The colour of sand you have chosen (see below) might dictate the planting. If you have chosen a plain, light-coloured sand, you will have a blank canvas that works with most plants, either foliage or flower led. If you have chosen a red sand, something rustic and traditional similar to what you'd find in a terracotta pot might work best. Using coloured sand makes the pot more of a feature, so you might want to keep your planting simple.
5. For a pretty finish, tie a ribbon or string around the pot.

Choosing your sand Sand comes in many colours and textures. Builder's sharp sand may be greyish, yellowish or reddish in colour, with bigger bits of grit in it. Kiln-dried sand is much paler and finer, which gives a much smoother effect. Or red sand can be used for a terracotta feel.

ROPED UP ⏱ A WEEKEND

YOU WILL NEED

Plastic pots
Superglue
Glue gun
Rope, string or wool
Paintbrush
Waterproof PVA glue
   (suitable for exteriors)

METHOD

1. The thinner the rope or string, the more times it will wrap around the pot so you'll need a longer length. Thicker rope or string needs a more generous dose of glue and maybe some hidden nails to hold in place. Wool can work nicely but make sure you coat it with waterproof PVA after it has been stuck onto the pot.

2. Apply super glue to the bottom edge of the outside of the pot.

3. Attach the string to the glued area so that it circles the pot. As you move up the pot, add glue to each layer you are about to wrap. Continue all the way to the top and over the rim so that the pot is completely covered.

4. Paint over the whole thing with waterproof PVA glue and leave to dry for up to 24 hours.

5. Plant up with something simple. In a small pot, a herbaceous perennial that has interesting foliage, like *Sedum*, *Phormium*, palms, *Pachysandra*, *Galium odoratum*, *Filipendula* will do very nicely. Deep colours like reds or purples mixed with little bits of silver can work really well. *Eryngium*, *Dianthus*, nasturtium, *Dahlia*, *Papaver*, *Lavandula*, *Fuchsia*, *Aster* and *Salvia* would all look beautiful.

The decorative nature of this pot lends itself to simple, foliage-led planting. Depending on the size of your pot you may want to use a fern or tree fern, a small shrub like *Ruscus*, *Hebe*, *Nandina*, *Skimmia* or a fruit tree like a blueberry.

MAINTENANCE

By now it will be clear to you that as a container gardener the onus is on you to keep your pots and plants looking good, but don't forget that a container is manageable – it is compact and controllable. Essentially, it's contained!

Every plant must really work hard and earn its place in your container, though, and that's also where you come in; they cannot be expected simply to sit there, doing their best, looking their prettiest, without a helping hand from you: a gentle nudge in the right direction, if you will. Your work is infinitesimally easier for containers kept outside, as the rain will water them for you and the sun will shine on them, but not bake them.

The biggest issue for you in their maintenance is that their true nature is being restricted. For example, a plant may only have a small 10cm cubed area of compost to feed from, year after year after year and yet it is expected to perform for you – to flower, to fruit, to produce more and more vegetation and give off delicious scents. It is up to you to make sure that the conditions in that small space give the plant everything it needs to thrive.

REFRESHING THE COMPOST

There are two key components to keeping a plant happy: nutrients, and moisture – without which the nutrients cannot be assimilated into a plant's roots. The compost holds both of these elements and, as one might expect, the quantities needed of each vary according to the particular plant.

The problem with compost in containers is that in a limited space the goodness from the compost gets used up fairly quickly, depending on the size of the container, and even if you are adding this through fertilisers, it is still a good idea to refresh the compost every year or two years.

It's not a tricky job, all you have to do is take the plant or plants out of the container, shake off the soil from the roots and set them aside, making sure the plants' roots don't dry out while they're out of the pot. You then need to remove the compost left in the pot (a little more challenging in a large pot!) and replace it with fresh compost. Once the pot is filled again, pot up the plants again and immediately water the newly composted pots so that the roots can make contact with the new compost.

It's a good idea to refresh the compost of outdoor containers in the winter, when the plants are dormant and therefore won't be hampered by the upheaval. If it is very cold, do this in a shed or garage (preferably somewhere unheated) rather than outside so that the roots don't freeze.

POTTING ON

Potting on is basically moving a plant from one, often smaller, pot to another, often larger, one. It is about replenishing the compost, but as well as refreshing the growing material, you are also increasing the space that a plant has by putting it into a bigger container.

Potting on needs to be done at different times depending on what you're growing and the stage of the plant's growth. If a plant has been happy for a long time in its container but begins to sicken, consider potting it on. However, before you do so, try reinvigorating it first with a new pot full of compost and see if that does the trick. If a plant looks really sad and should naturally be a large species, or if it starts to topple over in the wind because it has become a bit top heavy, go straight to the potting on.

A seedling will need potting on regularly. It should be 'pricked out' (gently removed from its pot using a dibber while holding one of the leaves) as soon as its true leaves (second set of leaves) form, then put into successively bigger pots as soon as the roots begin to show through the holes at the base of the original container. An annual plant, for example, tends to be bigger and better the larger the container that it's in. In a hanging basket, pot the seedling from a plug straight into its final position and let it grow to fill its space, but for most other containers, put a plant you have grown from seed into successively bigger versions until it's in its final pot.

For slower-growing plants or plants that you have grown from seed but are now mature specimens, repotting needs to happen far less often. As a container gardener, choosing the size of container gives you control over the growth of your plants. It is certainly not a matter of life and death if you do not pot on your plants – quite the opposite – you need to decide whether or not you want your plants to express their true nature (as they will in as big a container as you can find), or whether you use the container to restrict and control their growth to make them better suit your needs. Also consider that some species (*Agapanthus* being the most notable) actually thrive in a restricted environment. The more root-bound, the better the flowers will be on your *Agapanthus* plants. Not only that but they do not like their roots being disturbed, so if you pot them on they will take some time to recover and may even not flower. (There are only a few examples of such plants. *Agapanthus* is the most noteworthy, and famous, example because these kinds of plants are few and far between, though nearly all alpines thrive with restricted roots.)

FEEDING

How much or how little you should feed your plants varies hugely from species to species. If you are growing plants to harvest and eat, they will generally require more feeding than other plants. See page 56 for specifics, but generally a fruiting or flowering plant will need a high dose of potash, a leafy plant will require nitrogen and a root plant will require phosphates.

The one thing to remember is that in a container any food that a plant gets, it gets from you. In nature, there are all kinds of mechanisms for providing plants with nutrients, which are lacking in the less-than-natural environment of a plant pot. In a raised bed there will be more nutrient availability and if that raised bed sits on earth in your garden rather than concrete, or similar, it will benefit even more from nutrients. Generally, though, as a container gardener it is up to you to make sure your potted plants are fed to the right level. It could be that annually replacing the compost will do the job for you. It may also be that you add a little manure to seep down through the compost and keep your plants in good health. This could well be all your containers require, but many of us grow floral, hardworking plants which can be a little hungrier.

I would recommend that you give your containers a reinvigoration of compost on an annual or biennial basis, and then, for cropping or flowering plants, add a slow-release fertiliser in the spring and then a liquid feed every couple of weeks throughout the growing season. Your containers may need more rigorous feeding or you may need far, far less, but research the requirements for the species you grow and remember that the rule of thumb is usually the smaller the container, the more you will need to do to keep the plants healthy.

CLEAN AS YOU GO

It sounds boring, but containers can be a bit of an annoyance if they become too dirty. They can trap leaves, dust and debris behind them and after sitting there a while, getting watered periodically, with soil falling down them, their exteriors can get a bit grubby, too. So get in there every few months and have a clean – you could just direct the hosepipe on to the container itself and the ground around it when you're watering, or you could move the containers and have a good sweep and a wipe down every six months or so. You will find that it will make the whole area look brightened, fresh and generally better.

WATERING

Water is essential for plant growth. All plants need some moisture, but how much depends on the species. In a temperate climate, plants require water every few days, but do remember that it is easier to kill a plant by watering it too much than by not watering it enough. The bigger the container, the less you have to water it, and you definitely do not want your plants to be sitting in water – if soil is permanently moist it becomes devoid of oxygen and toxic to plants. Bog plants and water plants are exceptions, as they have evolved adaptations that enable them to deal with these conditions.

Generally you are aiming for a moist but free-draining environment that gives the plants just enough moisture. If you make a plant work hard for its moisture it will be tougher in the long run and will rely less on water than one that gets a good drink every day.

AUTOMATIC WATERING SYSTEMS

We've all been away on holiday or for work and suddenly realised that our beloved plants have been left without any water and may all be wilting, if not dead, on our return. It's heartbreaking to get home and see all of your precious progeny lying flat on their shrivelled brown faces on their parched, baked soil. But worry not, there are some little tricks I've learnt to avoid this devastation.

- Shoe laces – A bottle filled with water with a shoe lace dipped in it (right to the bottom) then pushed into the soil of each individual pot releases a slow drip feed to your plants.

- An irrigation system – For those with a little money to spend, this guarantees that there is always moisture in the soil. They even come solar powered, or they can be connected to water butts, or they can measure the moisture contents of the soil so that they only water when they need to. Clever stuff.

- An upturned bottle – Fill a bottle with water and stick it upside down in the soil. You can either remove the lid completely or make a little hole in the lid to release the water into the soil, depending how slowly you want the water to be released.

- Drip trays – Always make sure you leave a little water, about 2.5cm, in the drip tray. That will give you an extra couple of days watering free.

- Leave your containers in the bath – When I'm away for a long time I bring my most prized pots inside, leave about 5cm of water in the bath and put the plants in there. It isn't a great idea for a long time, but for a week or so it's a lifeline.

- Leave them outside – I mean, there's at least a 50:50 chance of rain, surely?

DEADHEADING AND CUTTING BACK

As with all plants, maintaining your container specimens to a high standard helps them perform better. Potted plants have to earn their space even more than plants in the rest of the garden because a container is a natural showcase. There are some basic things to remember to help you do this.

The first is deadheading – cutting the dead flowers off the plants. This may not be necessary with all species – some repeat flower, others don't; some produce fruit and seeds, others don't. So get to know your species. Certain plants will produce flowers prolifically according to how much you deadhead (think sweet peas, cosmos, dahlias and most other types of bedding), while some need the spent flowers left on in order to perform some other function, be it fruit or seed or hips. There is absolutely no point in spending hours deadheading when there is no need, but for those plants that do respond well to this treatment, it is an essential bit of maintenance. A little time spent snipping off the old flowers means that your containers won't be full of browning, messy old flower heads, and will also increase the flowering window of your plants, helping them to earn their place in your garden.

Another important job for container-grown plants is pruning. Again, how much or how little varies considerably according to what you've planted. A bonsai, for example, will need to be pruned by the roots and only on the top to remove dead branches, whereas a box hedge will need pruning once or twice a year, removing the tips and reshaping, and a herbaceous perennial will need to be cut back right to the ground during the winter. But there are a few hard and fast rules that can guide you here (see right).

HOW TO PRUNE

- Cut away any part of the plant that is dead, dying or diseased.

- Remove crossing branches on any shrub, to encourage an open habit (this allows air to circulate around the plant and prevents diseases taking hold).

- Generally, though not in every single case (*Clematis*, *Wisteria* and silver birch being common exceptions), prune plants once they have finished flowering.

- For coppicing, remove a third of the length of the stems every year. That way, every three years you will have replaced the whole tree with fresh new growth.

- Use sharp secateurs or loppers and ALWAYS clean them with disinfectant before you cut to prevent spreading diseases.

- Always cut just above a bud.

- Always cut the stem of the plant on the diagonal so that water does not sit on the wound.

CROP ROTATION

Crop rotation comes up time and again in gardening, and in a containers, of course, the problems you encounter in the ground are intensified unless you change the soil or compost every year.

Many of us grow vegetables in containers but we also often grow the same species year after year, particularly if they were successful before. It is an age-old problem: we like a vegetable, we don't have much space to grow it so we buy a container or build a raised bed. With such a small amount of space, why would we want to grow things we don't like as much? However, crop rotation in edibles is essential, and this may mean growing a few crops that aren't on your initial wish list. I'm speaking from experience; I got given a lot of brassicas and, even though I had grown them the previous year, I just bunged them in my raised bed again. I could hardly harvest any of them. As the year progressed, the cabbage root fly became more and more problematic. And the aphids were rampant. Luckily there was no club root in the soil or I would have had to wait 20 years or changed the whole lot. So my advice is – it's not worth it. Grow different plants in each container every year and you will have a much greater success rate.

It's also great for biodiversity to mix things up a bit. It keeps pests down, makes the crops perform better, prevents soil erosion, keeps weeds at bay and has even been suggested to increase the amount of oxygen produced by plants.

So in short, if you start right, plant right, feed right, water right, maintain your containers in the right way and don't always plant the same plants in the same place, then you should have containers that are not only beautiful, but functional and, crucially, that keep on giving year after year. Isn't it worth that little bit of thought and effort?

A simple Rotation Plan for Optimal Crop Health:

LEAF
Brassicas (cabbage, kohlrabi, broccoli, sprouts, kale), chard, spinach, etc.

ROOT
Potatoes, parsnips, carrots, beetroot, radish, turnip, celeriac, etc.

LEGUME
Beans, peas, mangetout, broad beans, lima beans, lentils, etc.

FRUIT
Tomatoes, aubergines, pumpkins, peppers, chillies, etc. (Can be substituted for grasses and *Alliums* – so sweetcorn, barley, onions, garlic, leeks, chives.)

INDEX

ACKNOWLEDGEMENTS

This book was a collaborative effort in so many ways and I am hugely indebted to the visionary people who created many of these beautiful containers. You all do a wonderful job and I sincerely hope you keep doing it for many years to come. Thank you for giving us a glimpse.

First and foremost I would like to thank Vicky Orchard and everybody at Kyle Books for giving me the opportunity to write this and turning my words into something I am hugely proud of. Second, to Rachel Warne, the most enormous thank you. Your photographs have brought this book to life and are more beautiful than I could have imagined. It was such a pleasure to work with you. Thank you also to Helen Bratby for the contemporary but beautifully tasteful design.

I would like to thank Ian Harris at Dawlish Gardens Trust. You have been a huge inspiration to me in my gardening work over the last few years and if one day I have brought half the happiness to half as many people as you have I will consider my time well spent. Thank you as well, and to Karen, for letting us take photos at DGT and giving me time off to write the book!

Thank you Steve Briers. For everything. Your house made a stunning backdrop to the photographs and a garden (and often house) filled with potted plants isn't always easy to live with! So thank you for your support and patience.

A big thank you must also go to Steve Edney, once again, for your generosity in giving us free rein at The Salutation as well as to Louise Dowell for letting us invade your own garden. What a beautiful space.

Thank you to Fergus Garrett for allowing us to photograph the spectacular displays at Great Dixter. They were an inspiration.

I would also like to thank Ken White at Frosts Landscapes for the fantastic locations around London, as well as Colin Evans, for being such a great guide and ever so patient!

To Martin Woods (mwgardendesign.co.uk) for showing us and letting us photograph your beautiful garden (a must-see for anyone interested in containers!) Thank you also to Shelley Hugh-Jones. Your designs were stunning and you were so helpful. Thank you to Claude Lester (vertigo.co.uk). Your potted roof terrace and green wall was fantastic. Thank you also to Francesca and Leandros at Langlea Garden Design. Also to Lahla Smart at Lahla Studios (lahlastudio.com) for the stunning magnetic pots. Thank you Mike Wateres at EZ Power steering UK (EZpowersteering.co.uk) for the visual feast of red and blue, and Tricia Kirkby at Garstone Garden Ornaments, Teignmouth, for letting us photograph one of my favourite living walls and the only historic boot living wall I know of! A big thank you for your advice about bedding plants and for the photographs to MJ and LP Disney and Olde Barn Gardens holiday cottages, Dawlish. Thank you to Toby's reclamation in Exminster. I would like to say a special thank you to Chris Britton at High Garden Nurseries, Kenton, for the beautiful plants. I hope they enjoyed their holiday by the sea... Thank you also to Sophie de Bouvier at Branching Out Antiques, Wingham, Kent and *Gardens Illustrated* and to The Original Hut company; The Hub, Bodiam, Kent for letting us feature photos of your lovely containers.

Thank you dad, for lending me your beloved bonsai, and driving us around the Kent and Sussex countryside in the rain. Thank you also to Bid and Mum for hunting out reclaimed containers (though I suspect you enjoyed it!)

Finally a huge thank you to Libby (Olivia Rhodes), Michael Hibberd, Michael Punnet, Brian Mills, Holly Maries and Laura Hunt for letting me invade your house and garden and build things – making a huge mess! You were all so welcoming and incredibly understanding.

Without all of your help this book could not have happened so thank you all so very much.